NELSON
MANDELA

A Force for Freedom

Dedication
For my elephant riders: bright-eyed Ben and my elegant Alexandra.

ISBN 978 0 233 00306 1
A catalogue record for this book is available from the British Library.

Design and editorial: Andy Jones, Ben Hubbard, Deborah Martin, Chris Gould

Printed in Dubai

NELSON MANDELA

A Force for Freedom

Christina Scott

ANDRE
DEUTSCH

CONTENTS

CHAPTER 1

"Girding for Battle"

The man known throughout the world as Nelson Mandela didn't exist by that name until some years after he was born.

It was instead a small boy named Troublemaker – a rough English translation of the vivid and poetic name Rolihlahla – who ran around the *mealie* (maize) fields among the tough goats and resilient adults, wrapped in earth-red blankets, who farmed the green inland valleys of the vast Transkei region down at the south-east tip of Africa.

The name chosen by his strict father suggests that the chief of the prosperous Mvezo village was a man of great vision who could see far into the future; for the tall nobleman's last-born son, Rolihlahla Nelson Mandela, certainly grew up to cause an enormous amount of trouble, for all the right reasons.

Mandela's astonishing path from protest to peace begins in a grim year of war and deadly sickness.

It was 1918 when Rolihlahla, or Troublemaker, was born in the small riverside village, where the evening cooking-smoke drifted over thatched round homes and dusty *kraals* (animal enclosures). The birth was significant only to his immediate family as this was the first (and only) son of Nosekeni, an aristocrat in her own right. Mandela's high-born father had older sons from his other wives, as was the norm in an extended rural family. Still, Chief Gadla Mphakanyiswa was delighted with his new son, and slaughtered a goat to notify the ancestors of the latest addition to a long-standing family.

While local midwives with a wide knowledge of useful herbs were assisting Nosekeni in her birth pangs, important leaders around the world were grappling with the huge changes that had been wrought by "the war to end all wars". In the same year, millions of people died in huge numbers from an invisible enemy, a particularly vicious mutation of the ordinary flu virus. "Influenza 1918" even became the title of a South African song, with its visionary lyrics crying out in Zulu that the virus, "Finished off our loved ones, our mothers and fathers, sisters and brothers. In some homesteads it finished off everyone: no one was left." The Mandela baby would grow up to see peace tarnished by the agonising deaths of many in Africa from another relentlessly transforming virus, HIV. And so "this old pensioner" as he mocks himself today, born in the midst of one global epidemic, now devotes his energies to fighting another.

1918 was a time when old men could still remember when they had ruled themselves, before refugees and settlers from Europe arrived in ships. The new addition to the extended Mandela family was considered fortunate because his father retained his inherited role as chief. A devout believer in the worship of the ancestors, Mandela's father was an honoured figure, a kind of lay minister, in the many events in this tight-knit rural community which marked the passing of the seasons and documented the cycle of life – births, deaths, marriages and ceremonies initiating the youth into adulthood. Praise-singers – oral historians with a flair for entertainment, analysis and humour – can trace the Mandela family back 20 generations, interwoven with the history of the Xhosa-speaking Thembu people, of the Transkei region. But to the white owners of South Africa, this proud family would have been considered a source of labour for the deepening gold mines, and little else.

A flock of grey crowned cranes graze beside the traditional Xhosa dwellings, or *rondavels*, in modern-day Transkei, Mandela's birthplace. There is no trace left of the original Mandela homestead today.

As the saying goes in South Africa, "When the whites came, we had the land and they had the Bible. They asked us to pray and when we opened our eyes, they had the land – and we had the Bible!" Soweto in 1992.

Almost immediately, while Mandela was just learning to crawl, financial disaster struck his affluent and influential family. To know why, you must understand that life in the rural Transkei was an uneven mixture of not one, but two fairly medieval systems.

People have been living in the Transkei for almost as long as there have been people: the very latest in genetic analysis indicates that the tiny, wiry Bushmen people who once roamed much of the southern nose of the continent are among the oldest continuous groups of human beings on this planet. In race-obsessed South Africa, Mandela's sharp cheekbones and deep-set eyes are often traced back to a group of Bushmen hunters known as the Khoikhoi.

Mandela's other ancestors were the Xhosa: resourceful cattle herders who slowly emigrated south in waves out of distant central Africa, at about the same time that the early medieval monarch Charlemagne was unifying France in Europe. As the pastoral people came over what are now known as South Africa's Dragon Mountains, the *Drakensberg*, they slowly developed a distinctive click language as they intermarried with the smaller, paler Khoikhoi

people. They settled in a vast rectangle of land stretching from the foothills of the mountains down to the waves of the Indian Ocean.

"Then our people lived peacefully, under the democratic rule of their kings and their *amapakathi* (counsellors) and moved freely and confidently up and down the country without let or hindrance," Mandela, the great-grandson of a king, would later say. "Then the country was ours, in our own name and right. We occupied the land, the forests, the rivers; we extracted the mineral wealth below the soil and all the riches of this beautiful country. We set up and operated our own government, we controlled our own armies and we organized our own trade and commerce."

There was no individual ownership of land in the Transkei, as in many pre-industrial societies. It belonged to the kings and was parcelled out in a fairly orderly fashion throughout their chiefs, administrators and advisers. However, following nine bloody frontier wars as land-hungry colonial-era settlers pushed up the coast from Cape Town from 1835 onwards, things changed in the Transkei forever. River by river, the Xhosa kingdoms shrank. At the end of this turbulent period, much of the best land was gone. As the saying goes in South Africa, "When the whites came, we had the land and they had the Bible. They asked us to pray and when we opened our eyes, they had the land – and we had the Bible!"

In a spooky foreshadowing of Mandela's own bitter experiences, the South African colonial authorities were able to seize some of the best military leaders of the region, such as the extraordinary Makhanda ka Balala – a prophet who angrily renounced his Christian upbringing after seeing his people in misery – a striking, military general who was the only commoner of his time to be granted aristocratic status.

Eventually, Makhanda gave up on military strategy, given the limited technology at his soldiers' disposal, and was willing to settle for peace, any peace, as his people were starving to death; their crops burning and their livestock perishing. Makhanda surrendered a century before Mandela was born, but both men share a strong link because Makhanda was imprisoned on a far-off, wave-tossed rocky island that was often known in isiXhosa as "Makhanda's island". We know it today as Robben Island, home to Mandela's cramped jail-cell for many years.

Old men's stories which enthralled young Mandela included that of the brilliant guerrilla leader Maqoma, who had been forced off his land three times before the British sent him and his wife to bleak Robben Island without a trial. For both of these early resistance leaders, the island was evil. It spelt death. A century later, Mandela would be walking in the footsteps of these men.

The Transkei hills and valleys slowly became the property of the British Empire, which did little to develop the region, or interfere with its residents, aside from offloading its surplus citizens there to farm, trade or preach. Then gold and diamonds were discovered in the arid plains or *veld* to the north. Overnight, southern Africa transformed from a dumping ground and a way-station to being a glittering prize in its own right. Britain fought two "white on white" wars against a tribe known as *die Boer*, or the farmer, stoutly Protestant descendants of Dutch and French victims fleeing murderous religious discrimination in distant Europe. They spoke a form of Dutch, heavily influenced by their slaves, which became known as Afrikaans.

While as many black South Africans died in the Anglo-Boer wars as Englishmen or Afrikaaners, this was not their war. It was a war about which group of whites would become rich from the precious metal shining dully in the chunks of rock. Now called the South African wars, the two clashes marked the world's first foray into truly modern warfare and left a bitter international legacy of concentration camps and guerrilla raids. Closer to home, the defeated Afrikaaners fumed but bided their time, waiting for an opportunity to gain total power, so they could have absolute protection for their people – the *Volk* – at any cost.

Meanwhile, when the British won their wars against the Afrikaaners in Mandela's father's lifetime, the empire did not erase the original Xhosa aristocracy. The traditional nobility was co-opted. The ruling power found that life was much easier if they made the monarchy and its network do their dirty work for them, in exchange for retaining their rights to land and cattle. And if the traditional nobility refused to co-operate, they could be removed. Someone else was always desperate for the job.

This system remained when eight years before Mandela's birth, the colony of South Africa became an independent country, although still part of the British empire. Chiefs uneasily served two masters: their traditional lords and the handful of oddly dressed white newcomers. Any whiff of rebellion –

... a far-off, wave-tossed rocky island that was often known in isiXhosa as "Makhanda's island". We know it today as Robben Island ...

Following page:
The prison on Robben Island had housed Mandela's childhood heroes, guerrilla leader Maqoma and prophet Makhanda ka Balala. A century later, Mandela would be walking in the footsteps of these men.

such as when the Zulu Chief Bambatha fought back in 1906 – was squashed as if the fighters were nothing more than lice crawling on a chicken.

The *amakhosi*, the chiefs, sometimes revelled in the illusion that they were in charge, but as Mandela's father's story shows, this was a mirage. A white magistrate sent a message summoning Mandela's father. He ordered "Henry" – his obligatory English name was so little-used that Mandela's father sometimes thought it must be Hendry – to appear before him about a trivial complaint.

The proud chief, as Mandela remembers in his memoirs, replied, "Andizi. Ndisaqula." "I will not come. I am girding for battle." The two systems, old and new, clashed. The father was charged with insubordination. Not considered important enough for a trial, he was promptly deposed and his land and cattle snatched away. He had been girding for a battle he could not win. Years later, his last-born son would be charged with a far more serious type of insubordination. It was called treason.

But for now Mandela was a small child named Rolihlahla, tied to his mother's back as she left her home and walked a few miles north on a footpath to a slightly larger village, Qunu, where she could count on family and friends to help her build a home, plant crops and raise her three children.

Mandela was too young to remember his more affluent beginnings. Qunu was home – and remains so to this day. His father, the former chief, would drop by regularly between visiting his other families. While Qunu might have been isolated from the wider world, this wasn't a solitary existence: the busy agricultural district bustled with relations, visitors and children.

The three Mandela *rondavels* – the distinctive round homes which dot the countryside – were handmade by his mother from soil shaped into bricks. One was used as kitchen and dining room, one was a bedroom and one served as storeroom. The child Rolihlahla wore a blanket dyed in red-ochre clay and needed no shoes or underwear. He ate pumpkins, beans, the African grain known as *sorghum* and the more recent Western import called corn or maize.

Mealies or corn cobs would be cooked for the main evening meal, the kernels ground to make a

> The proud chief ... was charged with insubordination. Not considered important enough for a trial, he was promptly deposed and his land and cattle snatched away. He had been girding for a battle he could not win.

kind of thick soup or mash, sometimes mixed with tart: soured milk from cows and goats. Meat came from the flock and was for festival days and celebrations. Tea and sugar were for the rich. Water came from the river. Light came from the sun or candles.

Although the system officially condemned adult Africans to lives as perpetual children, by the age of five Rolihlahla Mandela was contributing to the family welfare by working as a herdboy, bringing sheep and calves to and from the common pastures. A sense of working with the community was instilled in the Mandela boy at an early age.

Rural life also gave him a taste for independence. His favourite game was stick-fighting, where he learnt strategy – when to fake an attack, when to lunge, and when to concede defeat. Often Rolihlahla would only see his mother again at nightfall. After they had shared their food from the iron pot, she would roll out the thin reed sleeping mats and they would rest without pillows on the floor of a round thatched home.

It was also a life that encouraged sharp eyes. Children did not learn by bothering their parents

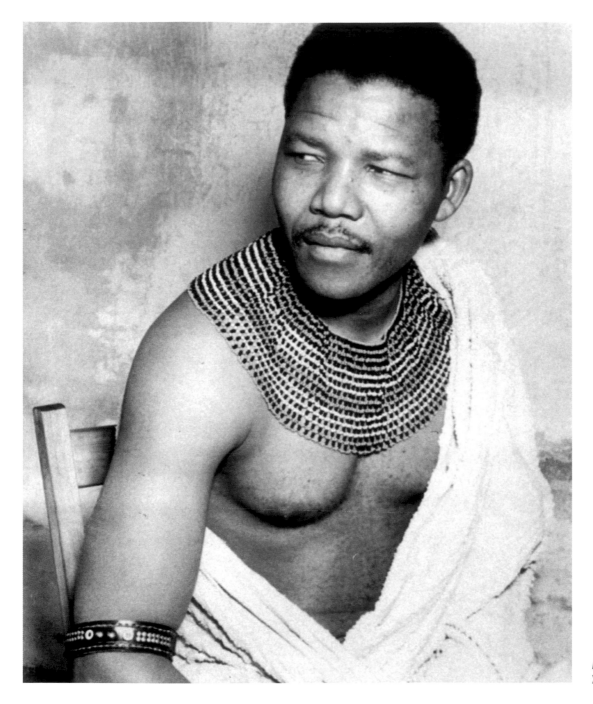

An older Mandela in traditional Xhosa dress.

with questions. Adults were always busy hoeing the fields, dousing tick-ridden livestock in the dipping tanks, cleaning the home, weeding the vegetable garden, digging out clay to make water pots. Children learnt from watching or from conversations with their peers, picking up signals along the way, which is how the child Rolihlahla knew without ever being told that the local whites – a magistrate and a shop-keeper – were to be treated with fear and respect. Why, he did not yet know.

In the village of Qunu, Mandela's pipe-smoking father befriended two brothers, both Christians, which was something of a rarity in this conservative world. The brothers never succeeded in converting Mandela's sceptical father but they made a great impression on his mother, who changed her name to

Fanny when she was baptised. Fanny's baptism may have led to the first great change in her son's life.

One of the brothers suggested that Rolihlahla should do something novel: attend school. This may well have been a way to gain another convert: the church-run school required all its students to be baptised first. Mandela's father, a great local historian who respected education of any kind, agreed to the request.

"My father took a pair of trousers and cut them at the knee," Mandela remembered. "He told me to put them on, which I did, and they were roughly the correct length, although the waist was far too large. My father then took a piece of string and drew the trousers in at the waist. I must have been a comical sight, but I have never owned a suit I was prouder to wear than my father's cut-off trousers."

Mandela in a suit – his "black Englishman" years. He would never feel prouder in a suit than in his first, with his father's cut-off trousers.

On his first day at school, the teacher insisted on giving him an unfamiliar English name: Nelson. But most languages in South Africa follow the vowel, syllable, vowel format so his mother rolled the strange sounds around her mouth and transformed the new word into "Nelisile." The new name seldom followed its owner outside the one-roomed schoolhouse with its unusual Western-style roof.

Beyond the school, Qunu was changing. Men were becoming a rarity. They needed money to pay government taxes levied on Africans only, so they boarded a distant train for the two-day trip to the mines in the centre of the country, where an ancient asteroid had split open the earth and thrown up an artery of gold near the surface. With the cash from a short-term contract, they could return to pay off the government and cover the school fees for children.

Many men stayed in the city, and forgot their families. Some vanished into the lawlessness. Mandela's father was one of the few who stayed. But two years later his father, coughing, died of what may have been tuberculosis. His son was nine. "I do not remember experiencing great grief so much as feeling cut adrift," Mandela would later remember.

Soon after completing their mourning rituals, Mandela was taken on a journey by his mother. They walked quietly through hills uncut by roads until by the end of the day they came to the most elaborate and impressive homestead the young boy had ever seen. This was the prosperous "Great Place", the hub of Thembuland. It was also the virtually self-sufficient royal residence of the wise Jongintaba Dalindyebo, a chief in his own right, who was acting as king on behalf of his young nephew.

Long ago, Mandela's father had recommended Jongintaba as regent because he was an educated man. Now it was 1927 and Jongintaba, a dapper Methodist with a predilection for handsome cars, was honouring his own responsibilities. He would become the adoptive father of the young Mandela, who would share a sparsely furnished *rondavel* with his own son, the fun-loving Justice Bambilanga.

It was another turning point. Mandela still loved his village. He still loved his mother and two sisters, who came to visit. Some of the other youngsters regarded him as a yokel who was hopelessly unequipped to exist in the rarefied atmosphere of the Great Place. But he suddenly realized that, "Life might hold more for me than being a champion stick-fighter." He might have joined the Church, one of the few ways open for Africans to progress economically. But the interim ruler had clearly indicated that his job was to follow in his late father's footsteps as a counsellor and advisor to royalty. It was not his decision. But he had no objections to his fate – not yet.

The shy country boy in the shabby clothes was hugely impressed by his foster father's style in everything from clothing to politics. He would carefully press the king's suits using an iron heated with coals. And he would listen attentively as any man, no matter how low-ranking, could strongly criticize the regent in public at communal meetings. There would be no interruptions or punishment. Jongintaba Dalindyebo let all speak their mind, but he would not speak his until he could detect some sort of unity or consensus. Mandela was also struck by the way the regent could speak with white policemen and magistrates and traders as if he were their equal. It did not occur to him that he could one day do the same.

A "slow and undistinguished" student, he attended several church-run schools where he scrawled the unfamiliar English words with chalk on a slate and made his first female friends. But one of the most important educational institutions for him was initiation school at the age of 16.

The regent had decided that both his own son, Justice, and his foster son, Nelson, were ready to become men. They needed to withdraw from society with other boys facing the same task. They had to attend a circumcision school, which would culminate in a significant rite of passage: each teenager would have his foreskin sliced off with one strike from an *assegai*, or spear, without anaesthetic, in front of a group of respected men.

"Ndiyindoda!" Mandela cried after that moment. "I am a man!" Once more, he was renamed, to mark the shift from child to adult. His proud new name was Dalibhunga, or the founder of the Bhunga, the traditional regional parliament. It was a prophetic name for a fighter for democracy. But the Bhunga

> "Life might hold more for me than being a champion stick-fighter."

was turning into a toy telephone: its members called out, but the government was not responding.

Many youths left school after being circumcised to marry, set up home and plough their own fields. But Mandela was meant to be a counsellor to kings, which required greater education. Since the government had no interest in educated black citizens, at the age of 19 he went away to another church-run college, Healdtown, where he found it mortifying to compete with others who were yet again smarter and more sophisticated. "I was a bit stuck-up in those days," he said ruefully. He was also still very provincial. Although he made his first non-Xhosa friend, he remembers being surprised that a teacher had married "out of his tribe".

His chief aspiration was to become a black Englishman. To that end the regent paid for him to enter the only university for black men (and women) in all of southern Africa. The famous University of Fort Hare had been founded two years before Mandela's birth by dour Scottish missionaries and would remain the only university for black students (unless they studied by correspondence course) until 1960. Afrikaaners were outraged at this blatant British meddling and mocked Fort Hare for providing an education for a society which did not exist. Competition from black South Africans was both denied, derided and feared at all levels of white society – so much so that a proposed training school for black domestic workers was once accused of forcing white women into prostitution.

Mandela had been encouraged to study law to help him best advise the young king-in-waiting but he was on the edge of outgrowing the Great Place. Instead, he rather fancied himself in a showier role: perhaps a court interpreter, or even a clerk with his

Xhosa boys during their initiation ceremony, which culminates in circumcision with a spear and no anaesthesia. A significant moment for a 16-year-old Mandela, who, following the procedure, cried out "Ndiyindoda!" ("I am a man").

own desk in the civil service's Native Affairs department.

"Nel" was 21 when he went to university, dashing in his first double-breasted suit, only to be promptly shot down by a senior student as "a backward fellow from the countryside" who "cannot even speak English properly". Other friendships were more rewarding, including that of a "serious young science student" by the name of Oliver Reginald Tambo. Tambo's diplomatic skills would play a critical role in Mandela's later life. While they were at university, they heard for the first time about an organization called the African National Congress (ANC), formed in 1912, and knew the ANC was campaigning for voting and land rights, but it made little impact. In Mandela's case, he was too busy studying, learning ballroom dancing steps, competing in cross-country racing and teaching Bible classes in surrounding villages on Sundays.

He wore pyjamas for the first time, finding them uncomfortable. He used toothpaste and toothbrush instead of a twig and ash, and discovered flushing toilets instead of long-drops. If he wanted to go over the river to eat in the small town of Alice, which wasn't very often because he had no spending money, the students would have to lurk around the

kitchen door. They knew it would cause a scandal to eat in the restaurant.

The tall athletic university student was no radical. He was horrified when his friend Paul Mahabane, the son of a former ANC leader, refused to grovel before a white man in the town of Umtata, some 22 kilometres from his home village, one holiday:

"We were standing outside the post office when the local magistrate, a white man in his sixties, approached Paul and asked him to go inside to buy him some postage stamps. It was quite common for any white person to call on any black person to perform a chore. The magistrate attempted to hand Paul some change but Paul would not take it."

The magistrate was furious, asking Mandela's friend, "Do you know who I am?"

"It is not necessary to know who you are," Mahabane snapped back. "I know what you are."

Mandela was "extremely uncomfortable". He was beginning to learn something not taught in textbooks. "I knew that if he had asked me rather than Paul, I would have simply performed the errand and forgotten about it."

The tiny university, which never went over 200 students, was schizophrenic. Politics and race shaped everything there but neither was discussed. The white man's war in Europe and Asia was

Mandela with Oliver Tambo, whom he met at university, where they both heard about the ANC for the first time. Tambo was quiet where Mandela was fiery, and together they would hijack the ANC, and change South Africa forever.

followed minutely – but his behaviour in Africa went unscrutinized. The lack of opportunities for Africans was like the sun coming up in the morning: no need to analyse it. The warren of rules and regulations and insults and inconveniences that made up racial oppression was not on the agenda. The chance to join the African elite, on the other hand, was constantly highlighted.

"I believed that the world would be at my feet," he said. It was a chance to buy his long-suffering mother a nice house and earn some money.

But Mandela didn't graduate from Fort Hare University as planned. Involved in the Students Representative Council, he was sent down for a year in a minor clash that saw him for the first time prioritizing his conscience over convenience. He had been nominated for the Students Representative Council, which then decided to boycott their own elections in protest at the inadequate diet, which was partly a deliberate effort to keep fees as low as possible. According to Oliver

Tambo, "What was called supper was four remarkably thin slices of bread, taken with a small cup of milk water, the water of which would be hot."

While others compromised when outwitted by the university administration, Mandela found that he could not compromise on an ethical issue. He was the only holdout: "Something inside me would not give."

The university authorities promptly said that any student resigning from the council would be expelled. Mandela objected to the principal's "absolute power over me" and didn't budge. "I had taken a stand, and I didn't want to appear to be a fraud."

His adoptive father was furious to see Mandela at home and announced that he would return to university in the autumn, join the Students Representative Council and soon graduate with his degree.

A few weeks later, Mandela's entire life changed course.

CHAPTER 2

"I Have Crossed
Famous Rivers"

Nelson Mandela was 23 and on the run for the first – but not the last – time in his life. The tall college student had fled his birthright as prime minister to kings in order to arrive with just one suitcase in a brash and noisy new city built quite literally on gold – and all because of a woman.

His adoptive father had been worried that he might pass away in these troubled times without seeing his beloved children settled. So Chief Jongintaba Dalindyebo had decided upon arranged marriages for both Mandela and his own son. But unbeknown to the chief, the young lady he had selected for Mandela was actually in love with his own son, Justice Bambilanga.

Justice objected. So did Mandela, who was four years younger. But he was told sharply that the *lobola* – or dowry, usually paid in cattle – had already been delivered to the family of the young lady concerned. All objections were useless. "He had made his decision and he was not going to alter it," Mandela said.

Mandela, a self-confessed romantic, was not in love; and this was important to him. But that was not all that troubled him about the situation. The stubborn, even arrogant, young man also refused to permit another human being to have control over him. As at university, he was almost physically unable to give in. He noted the irony: "While I would not have considered fighting the political system of the white man, I was quite prepared to rebel against the social systems of my own people."

The two young men tried to run away but needed money, so they stole two of the regent's prize-winning oxen and deceived a local trader into believing that they were selling the beasts on the old man's behalf.

With the profits, they secretly hired a car and driver to take them to the nearest railway station, impatiently planning to decamp for Johannesburg – a bustling boom town which had sprung up within the last five decades from a tented mine camp.

But Jongintaba Dalindyebo outsmarted them. "Your father has been here and says you are trying to run away," the manager of the railway station announced. The chief had taken the precaution of warning the local stationmaster that two young men of their description should not be issued tickets.

At any minute, the chief might be contacted. So the astonished duo rushed back into their hired car and offered the indifferent driver almost all the money they had to take them more than 50 miles away to the next station, where they caught the next train.

The two cocky young men very nearly didn't make it out of Queenstown, the administrative centre of a prosperous farming district. Both systems of authority, colonial and traditional, hemmed in the would-be rebels at every turn. For a start, they were handicapped by the notorious pass laws, which required all African men over the age of 16 to carry an internal passport. This pass, or *dompas*, had to be frequently updated with stamps and papers indicating that the men were allowed to move around a particular magisterial district – but only for a set time and only for a specific purpose. It also had to show that they had paid their poll tax, a levy that white South Africans did not have to pay.

Anyone whose employer went bankrupt, whose magistrate filled in the wrong date or whose

For a black South African in Johannesburg, insult and indignity were a daily experience.

NELSON MANDELA

traditional leader refused to co-operate, faced constant arrest, trial, jail and fines. It was a brilliantly bureaucratic technique for making black South Africans prisoners in their own country. Mandela couldn't very well ask the chief to organize the correct travel documents and permission, so he was officially illegal. Trying to remedy this, the two rascals had some spectacularly bad luck. Still in

Queenstown, they lied to a prominent uncle, with good connections at the local court, who thought he was helping out the very same regent from whom they had fled. However, just as the local white magistrate stamped their papers, he realized that as a matter of common courtesy, he ought to debrief the chief magistrate in their home district.

"Oh, their father just happens to be right here," said the helpful magistrate in Umtata, Transkei. He handed the phone over to Jongintaba Dalindyebo, who erupted with fury.

"Arrest those boys!" came down the line, loud and clear. "And bring them back here immediately!"

They were not arrested because Mandela used what little knowledge of the law he had acquired in order to stand up to the magistrate, who called the two thieves and liars. It was one of the first times in his life he had openly successfully stood up to authority of almost any kind. It worked. Without realizing it, Mandela was preparing himself for far bigger clashes with authority.

Meanwhile, a distant friend who knew that his white employer's mother was driving to Johannesburg organized that they pay for the privilege of sitting in the back seat. The cost of hitching a lift used up the rest of their savings before they even reached Johannesburg where somehow, they fixed or faked their despised documents later. The year was 1941.

"A vast landscape of electricity," was Mandela's jubilant first reaction on seeing Johannesburg. "A city of light."

But his prospects were dark. In the 1940s, many similar refugees from the drought-stricken countryside formed a citywide network of friends and relatives; an informal welfare net in the face of a hostile government. Such a network was an

The city of gold. "A vast landscape of electricity," was Mandela's jubilant first reaction on seeing Johannesburg. "A city of light."

absolute necessity for survival in gangster-ridden Johannesburg. But Mandela and his adoptive brother Justice had cut themselves off from their community through their deceit. It was a hard lesson to learn.

In the city of gold, or *Egoli*, Mandela very nearly became a miner. "Miners had a mystique," he said. "To be a miner meant to be strong and daring: the ideal of manhood." Although young men boasted of the glamour of the work, in reality it was incredibly dangerous.

Fortunately, his first job was above ground as a guard at the city's largest gold mine, routinely checking the paperwork of workers next to a large sign warning "Beware: Natives Crossing Here." That is, until the tough *induna*, or mine headman, received a telegram from the Transkei. "Send boys home at once," the chief ordered.

But instead of returning home, Mandela drifted from job to job, never holding one for long because he kept lying about his clash with the deeply respected chief. Sooner or later, the "homeboy" grapevine, which knitted together urban and rural South Africa, would spring into action and he would be exposed, disgraced and fired. Often he would also be asked to leave the backyard shack he was renting or be forced to abandon the mine hostel accommodation.

Mandela was written off as a failure. He had no money, no job and no connections. He had been tossed out of university. His father was long dead, his mother was poor, and he had now started a family feud with his traditional leader.

Johannesburg didn't care that he was the descendant of kings. Johannesburg didn't care that he had studied at one of the finest universities on the continent. Johannesburg was interested in two things: skin colour and money. These, and these alone, conferred power.

Mandela's luck took a turn for the better when the disgraced university student found his way through a sympathetic cousin to the busy downtown offices of kind-hearted Walter Sisulu, a quiet, calm, real estate agent who hailed from the same region of the country, the Transkei, and spoke the same language, Xhosa.

Still a conservative country boy, Mandela remembered in his memoirs being deeply impressed by the fact that Sisulu had an African woman working for him as a typist: "I had never seen a black man in an office, let alone running an estate agency. I did not even know what an estate agency was."

He also noted how well Sisulu communicated in a language that was not his mother tongue. Despite a university education, his own English was laborious and stiff. Mandela, speaking to Sisulu, once again glossed over the truth about his family rift.

Seeing the potential in this lanky, badly dressed country bumpkin, Sisulu arranged for him to be taken on as an articled clerk – a kind of legal apprentice – in a local white lawyer's firm, on condition that he finish his Bachelor of Arts degree by studying at night through correspondence university. In the meantime, the law firm, one of the largest in the city, could use Mandela as a clerk and a messenger and that way he could pay for his university studies. Of course, this meant that he would have almost no money left for living expenses – but he didn't care. The chance to become a lawyer! A job at a lawyer's firm!

The lawyers, on the other hand, "did not seem very keen on me," Mandela later wryly said. But Walter Sisulu "was one of their important clients

Johannesburg didn't care that he was the descendant of kings. ... Johannesburg was interested in two things: skin colour and money. These, and these alone, conferred power.

"Miners had a mystique," Mandela said. "To be a miner meant to be strong and daring: the ideal of manhood." In reality it was incredibly dangerous.

who brought them business". They could not say no.

Sisulu was not acting on impulse. Despite the typist in the front room, a waiting room full of clients and a desk full of papers, he was no mere businessman – his real job was not real estate but the human estate. Sisulu was a few years older than Mandela. He had been born in the same year that the ANC had been formed, 1912, and his life was entwined with this institution's struggle for human rights. His absent father was white, and Sisulu would often have found life far easier if he had registered himself as a coloured, or a person of mixed race, but as a man of great personal integrity, he always refused the easy way out.

Mandela was not the only casualty of university expulsions who found his way to Johannesburg and to Sisulu's busy offices. Another fatherless, poor, but bright student, Oliver Tambo, the deeply religious, thoughtful teetotaller whom Mandela had first met at Fort Hare, was also later gently pushed by Sisulu to become a lawyer. Tambo and Mandela would soon form Johannesburg's first black law firm. They would also sit side by side in the treason trial – as accused, rather than as defence lawyers.

Sisulu later told Tambo's biographer Luli Callinicos that whenever he came across a bright young man, he would encourage him to take up law. The law was an important weapon in the struggle; a struggle that many barely even knew of yet. The lives of all three would be linked at every possible level in ways that none of them could yet foresee. In many ways, these two relationships with Sisulu and Tambo lasted longer than any of Mandela's three marriages. They were to form an inseparable trio,

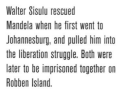

Walter Sisulu rescued Mandela when he first went to Johannesburg, and pulled him into the liberation struggle. Both were later to be imprisoned together on Robben Island.

Oliver Tambo in his and Mandela's law offices. With Sisulu, Tambo and Mandela became the inseparable trio, forming a triumvirate which could resist anything but death.

even when physically barred by prison walls and exile across oceans – a triumvirate, which could resist anything but death.

But shortly after Mandela's visit, Walter Sisulu received a stern warning from the then leader of the ANC, a man with close links to traditional leadership, instructing him not to assist Mandela or his fellow fugitive, Justice, and explaining the full circumstances of their disgrace.

But these were not the rolling green hills of the Transkei, anchored in tradition, but the skyscrapers of Johannesburg, where rules were made to be broken. Walter Sisulu may have been a loyal ANC follower but he chose to ignore the ANC instruction – and in doing so, he may have changed the course of history.

In fact, Sisulu did more than keep close ties with Mandela, arrange his first job, lend him the money to buy a suit for his first graduation, and introduce him to his first love. The advantage of being poor in a get-rich-quick city was that at least "Nel" learnt who his true friends were. The Sisulu family, including Walter's supportive sister and mother, also provided a home for Mandela for several months – a real find in one of the rare housing developments for black South Africans in Johannesburg during the war years.

This was in Orlando West, in what would eventually grow to become the vast sprawl of Soweto, short for South-western township. Although Soweto claims him as its son today, Mandela feels that the township of Alexandra, to the north of the growing city, was his real home.

In both places, virtually every back yard became packed with the shacks and shanties of tenants as the housing shortage for black South Africans grew worse and worse. Mandela and many others were forced to rely on outside toilets using the bucket system, in which a man with a horse-drawn cart buzzing with flies would remove the sewage. He would also have to rely on outside communal water taps. Johannesburg found it very easy, in a multitude of ways, to make life difficult for its black workers.

Mandela's clothes remained so threadbare that stylish gangsters disliked sitting next to him on the Alexandra bus. He needed candles to study at night because he could not afford the paraffin for a lamp. But hope was in the air as the city was busy reinventing itself yet again, this time from a mining metropolis into the largest manufacturing source on the continent. War clouds loomed as Europe went to war again. South Africa had declared war on Germany in 1939, and hundreds of thousands of South Africans were making a multiracial contribution to the war effort in Africa and Europe.

In Johannesburg, Mandela was still coming out of what he calls his "black Englishman" phase, so when the shy young man attended his first mixed-race party, he desperately hunted for a tie so he could appear respectable. "There will always be, in emerging nations, an enduring attraction to the ways of the colonizer," he later confessed. "I myself was not immune to it."

It was a shock to realize that this particular group didn't care about his dress code. They were communists. But young Mandela remained suspicious of whites, both Afrikaans and English-speaking, who believed in racial equality. He was religious; communists were not. Not that all the communists at the party were white; some were classified as coloured, a term which in South Africa applied to both the children of mixed-race marriages and the offspring of Malaysian-Muslim aristocrats exiled to Africa by the Dutch colonizers centuries earlier. Others at the party were classified as Indian, the descendants of indentured labourers shipped out by the British to work under appalling conditions in the sugar-cane fields along the country's east coast.

The two faces of 1940s Johannesburg – "the New York of Africa": a prosperous city of art deco apartments contrasted with native dwellings made of burlap and corrugated iron.

Mandela had met both coloured and Indian students at Fort Hare, but had formed no close relationships in such a heavily segregated society. He was wary. But once he made a commitment to life – and politics – across the colour bar, it would be unshakeable. Meanwhile, urban life in hectic Johannesburg, where gold miners came from all over southern Africa, rendered Mandela less tribal. When greeting the acting queen of the baSotho people, his seSotho was so bad that she snorted, "What kind of lawyer and leader will you be who cannot speak the language of your own people?" He had unconsciously given in to the tribalism emphasized by the white government. He began to see that the insistence amongst the ruling whites that tribes were separate from each other was a divide-and-rule plan.

In 1941 Mandela made peace with friends and family in the distant Transkei. He reconciled with the regent but made no plans to return. He didn't have to reconcile two worlds of city and countryside, like many migrant workers, because in many ways he had chosen urban over rural.

Other friends with rural roots argued against this approach, pointing out that Johannesburg had plenty of educated Africans in comparison and that it was the rural areas that needed people of his calibre. Later, his first wife would never give up hope that he would abandon politics and return to the Transkei.

But Mandela's legal mind identified this option as a trap, a dead end. No matter how much he might improve the lot of his extended family or the broader community of the Transkei, as long as black South Africans were oppressed elsewhere, any improvement would be cosmetic.

1942 was a momentous year. His father figure and traditional ruler, the clever Jongintaba Dalindyebo, died that year. Mandela also finished his first degree, the Bachelor of Arts course he had begun under very different circumstances at Fort Hare College in the Transkei. Now, he could take articles to be a lawyer.

Mandela's legal job was a demeaning one but it did open up new opportunities. His only other black colleague was Gaur Radebe, a sardonic,

Johannesburg, 1957: Black taxi drivers jam the roads, angered by the frequent police checks owing to one of the bus boycotts. The earlier 1943 bus boycott in Alexandra, which included Mandela, lasted nine days.

multilingual communist and a committed activist who coached him in the ways of the city – and the need for a change. Like Sisulu, he took the country boy to political debates.

Eventually the two of them marched with ten thousand others in support of the nine-day-long Alexandra bus fare boycott in 1943. African people were not allowed to live in the city centre, or anywhere near places of work, so public transport ate a huge hole in the most carefully managed budgets – including that of Mandela when he lived in Alexandra. "On many days I walked the six miles to town in the morning and the six back in the evening in order to save the bus fare."

The bus boycott would work. "In a small way, I had departed from my role as an observer and become a participant," Mandela said. "I found that to march with one's people was exhilarating and inspiring."

Politics and law were coming closer together. He also enrolled at Wits – the University of the Witwatersrand – for the next stage in his legal training, a Bachelor of Law degree, during which time he met for the first time white South Africans of his own age. University life felt odd. Here, in the land of his birth, he was considered a token, an exotic. In addition, he noted critically, "my performance as a law student was dismal".

In the same year as the bus boycott, in an astonishing act of personal generosity, Gaur Radebe actually resigned his job at the legal firm.

"My boy, as long as I am here at the firm, they will never article you, whether or not you have a degree," he said. Mandela disagreed.

"They will not tell you this to your face; they will just postpone and delay," Gaur replied. "It is important to the future of our struggle in this country for you to become a lawyer and so I am going to leave the firm and start my own estate agency. When I am gone, they will have no choice but to article you."

He left. Mandela eventually was articled, as promised.

Not all the staff were so supportive. When

Mandela graduated to a more senior level, white secretaries were so embarrassed about being seen taking dictation from him that one woman ordered him out on a personal errand when they were interrupted.

"I left the room and got her shampoo," Mandela said. The firebrand who would order policemen to call him Mr Mandela when they were arresting him was not yet in existence.

The constant *klaps* – slaps – administered by Johannesburg may have been good in a way. Confronted with insults and indignities every day, Mandela could hide in the faded glories of the pre-settler past, or drown himself in drink, or he could do something about the present.

He did something about the present. He joined the African National Congress. In it, he found another home, one that would sustain him for the rest of his life. As the saying goes in Mandela's mother tongue, "Ndiwelimilambo enamagama" – "I have crossed famous rivers" – meaning, "I have travelled far".

For Mandela, his travels were just beginning.

The next year, the ANC began to shrug off its old-fashioned behaviour, under the impatient influence of men like Sisulu, Tambo and Mandela. It discarded the House of Chiefs that had given special status to hereditary leaders. It reluctantly allowed women to join on an equal footing to the men. And for the first time, it called for one person, one vote, instead of its previous suggestions of agonizingly slow, gradual improvements in voting rights.

But some things didn't change. The ANC, although it was lobbying the government for change, still had government officials open their conferences, who often used the occasion to urge the "natives" to be patient.

It wasn't enough for Mandela. A year later, he and select group of angry young men presented the ANC with a ready-made constitution for a related body known as the Youth League. Despite grumblings from the old guard, the inaugural conference of the Youth League was allowed to go forward on Easter Sunday, 1944. Their manifesto explicitly rebelled against the idea that whites

The Youth League, 1944: Mandela, Sisulu and Tambo felt the ANC was bogged down in a useless cycle of pleading and begging. This was the route to the future – militant and activist.

somehow had black interests at heart. The Youth League was going to bring protest politics to South Africa.

His personal life improved as well: he developed a reputation for being a ladies' man.

Perhaps it was the marrying season. Mandela certainly seemed to be infected by the happiness of his close friend Walter Sisulu when he began dating Albertina Ntsiki Thethiwe, a nurse.

At the bustling Sisulu house, his eye fell on a quiet Sisulu relative, Ntoko Evelyn Mase. Evelyn was an orphan whose mineworker father had died when she was an infant, followed by her mother when Evelyn was 12. She had left the Transkei, where the government baulked at building or staffing secondary schools for black students, in order to complete her education.

Her aunt, Walter Sisulu's mother, took both Evelyn and her older brother under her wing and into their tiny house, and she was now training under Albertina at the Johannesburg general hospital's strictly segregated non-European section.

After a whirlwind courtship, Mandela tied the knot with the pretty young girl from his home region at the beginning of 1944. "I asked Evelyn out very soon after our first meeting," Mandela said. "Almost as quickly, we fell in love. Within a few months, I had asked her to marry me, and she accepted."

Later that year, Mandela was best man when Walter Sisulu paid the *lobola*, or bride-price, and married Albertina. One of the speechmakers at the Sisulu wedding warned Albertina that she was committing a kind of polygamy, because she was marrying a man already married to the nation. Shared politics would cement the Sisulu marriage, so similar to the Mandelas' in many respects. But politics would eventually drive Evelyn away from her husband.

After staying with a series of Evelyn's relatives, the couple were reluctantly allowed permission to rent a tiny government house in a distant blacks-only suburb because they had their first son, Madiba Thembekile, known as Thembi, a "solid, happy little boy", according to his proud father.

"The house itself was identical to hundreds of others built on postage-stamp-sized plots on dirt roads," is how Mandela described it. "It had the same standard tin roof, the same cement floor, a narrow kitchen and a bucket toilet at the back."

The bedroom was so small that a double bed took up almost all the space. There was no electricity yet, although there were street lamps outside. They shared the tiny matchbox house with Mandela's younger sister Leabie, who also took the two-day train ride from the Transkei in order to finish her high school education, with a succession of homeless visitors, their spouses and children. "I enjoyed domesticity, even though I had little time for it," Mandela said. "I love playing with children and chatting with them; it has always been one of the things that makes me feel most at peace."

But peace – personal, professional or political – was not on the horizon.

In 1947 Mandela completed his articles and resolved to become a full-time law student to speed up the time until he could be an attorney. His pregnant wife supported her husband and son financially through nursing but then lost the frail and sickly daughter, Makaziwe, at the age of nine months.

"Evelyn was distraught," Mandela remembered. He threw himself into his studies and the expansion of the ANC, returning home late at night and staying away most weekends.

In 1948, an election loomed. "Africans could not vote, but that did not mean that we did not care who won," Mandela pointed out. The ruling party was led

The young lawyer. Mandela would soon be swapping his double-breasted suit for a series of disguises, including a chauffeur's uniform and gardener's overalls.

> "I enjoyed domesticity, even though I had little time for it," Mandela said. "I love playing with children and chatting with them; it has always been one of the things that makes me feel most at peace."

NELSON MANDELA

by General Jan Smuts, a man who had clashed bitterly with Gandhi over South Africa and had done nothing to advance black rights, but was held in high regard in North American and European diplomatic circles.

The contenders were the Nats. The National Party, which publicly sympathized with Nazi Germany, had put up posters warning in Afrikaans about the *swaart gevaar* – the black danger – and said that Afrikaaners were God's chosen people. The posters advocated that they would put the *kaffir* and the *coolie* – grossly insulting terms for blacks and Indians – in their proper place. Their proper place, it turned out, was at the bottom of a system of social control known as apartness. In Afrikaans, it was called apartheid. Hundreds of years of informal social segregation was about to move up a notch. Mandela called apartheid bureaucracy: "Diabolical in detail, inescapable in its reach and overwhelming in its power."

General Smuts might have been able to defeat the Nazis but he lost to the Nats by five seats. Mandela was taken by surprise. His soft-spoken colleague Oliver Tambo, even though he had been accosted by an angry white male on voting day who spat in his face, took a more long-term view. "I like this," he told the stunned Mandela. "Now we will know exactly who our enemies are."

The government set to work with a vengeful energy, bent on eliminating every vestige of English rule. Nazi sympathizers were released from jail. Trade unions were strangled. Every person had to be classified by race. The handful of coloured, Indian or African people who had somehow managed to get their names on the voters' roll were kicked off. Both sex and marriage between the races were made criminal offences. Each race group had to have its own suburbs, its own schools, its own transport – although naturally, the white race group got the pick of the lot. Everything from

Sophiatown in the 1950s. Mandela wanted the ANC to change its tactics from feeble protest petitions to something more along the line of Gandhi's passive resistance campaign in India.

well-paying jobs to park benches and beaches were marked for the exclusive use of whites. Families were broken up along racial grounds, depending on the results of pencil tests to determine the kinkiness of your hair or the callipers to measure the thinness of your lips.

In response, Mandela wanted the ANC to change its tactics from feeble protest petitions to something more along the line of Gandhi's passive resistance campaign in India. One of his former professors called him "a naïve firebrand". Some of the most senior members of the ANC described him as arrogant and disrespectful.

Nonetheless, in a conference in Bloemfontein, one of the most conservative cities in the country, the Youth League routed the old guard. Mandela could not savour the success because he was working for a new law firm that would have fired him for taking days off in pursuit of politics. Politics, thus far, occupied only his free time – even though he now served on the national executive of the ANC.

If the government had been reasonable, perhaps it would all have ended there. After all, Mandela didn't even particularly enjoy being a political leader. It was more fun being a dissident. Now he could expect to be criticized by activists even more rebellious than he was.

But the government was not reasonable. In 1950, Mandela had had his first baptism of fire – ironically, for a protest he had opposed. It was a stay-at-home strike against all the new and viciously discriminatory legislation, organized by a multiracial coalition of communists and Gandhi-inspired Indian activists, and he hadn't learnt to trust such colleagues yet. Police monitoring the one-day strike – in which two-thirds of all the African workers stayed at home – noticed the distinctive outline of the tall Mandela with much shorter Walter Sisulu, watching a crowd that had gathered in defiance of a ban on all meetings. They fired.

"We dived to the ground and remained there as mounted police galloped into the crowd, smashing people with batons," Mandela said. Although the news barely made the main newspapers, 18 protestors died and many more were injured.

He was outraged. He remained outraged when the government then responded to the communist

His five-year-old son Thembi plaintively asked his mother, "Where does Daddy live?"

protest by banning the party in words so vague that almost anyone lobbying for change could have gone to jail. In response, he called for something historic: a united front against apartheid.

Mandela also called for the first nationwide ANC strike on political issues, in protest against both the 18 dead and the clampdown on communists. In the middle of organizing the strike, known as the Day of Protest, in March 1950, his wife gave birth to their second son, Makgatho Lewanika. Mandela was at the hospital for the birth, but left soon afterwards. His five-year-old son Thembi plaintively asked his mother, "Where does Daddy live?"

In 1951, Mandela was ready to become an independent lawyer. One of his first acts was to break the law. He persuaded an Indian owner to quietly let him occupy his offices in the only accessible part of the city. Within a year, the frosted windows read "Mandela and Tambo" in large gold letters. What the windows didn't reveal was that in the same year, the highly visible Mandela was restricted to Johannesburg by the government: the first banning order in an endless series of restrictions.

Mandela continued to meet with activists on the sly, helping teams prepare a series of protests, which made no impact on the government or the voters. In the courtroom, he was unavoidable, a vivid, prominent figure who didn't behave in the humble manner demanded of blacks. Instead, Mandela strode in like the royalty he was, upright and dashing in tailored suits and white silk scarves. There was a "hint of arrogance around him which wasn't really arrogance", explained Lancelot Gama, another student expelled from Fort Hare who became active in the struggle. Mandela's posture, his voice, his body "was for him an instrument to hit at this system. To say, 'Look, I am as equal with you

as with anybody else in this courtroom. We speak the same language; we are addressing the same issues. I am not inferior to you.'"

Mandela's close friend Oliver Tambo had to travel around the country, as their desperate clients came from every corner of South Africa. Tambo, a scholarly intellectual by temperament, dogged by asthma, didn't mind. He had already recognized that Mandela was "a born leader". In a book of Mandela's speeches compiled by Ruth First, an activist later assassinated by the South African security police in Mozambique, Tambo described his friend: "Nelson Mandela is passionate, emotional, sensitive, quickly stung to bitterness and retaliation by insult and patronage. He has a natural air of authority. He cannot help magnetising a crowd: he is commanding with a tall handsome bearing; trusts and is trusted by the youth, for his impatience reflects their own; appealing to women. He is dedicated and fearless. He is the born mass leader."

Mandela in the law office he shared with Oliver Tambo. Theirs was the first black law practice in Johannesburg.

While the law was an avenue of protest, the legal work of Mandela and Tambo seldom broke new ground. Mandela found he could only gain people a brief breathing space before the government found a way to block their loophole. They were reduced to defending desperate clients, who crowded the chairs in the waiting room and overflowed into the corridors, or take matters on appeal. Police watched who entered the building – watched, and waited.

"You are a young attorney, you're doing so well," pleaded the white legal conveyancer who took on Tambo as an articled clerk. "You are getting yourself so involved in politics it's going to affect your future."

"I've reached the stage in my life when I can't make my own decisions," replied Oliver Tambo, who always shunned the limelight. "I am going with the current, and the current is carrying me with Nelson Mandela."

CHAPTER 3

"The People Shall Rule!"

If the government wouldn't listen to the people, Mandela would. The African language of seSotho has a motto "Kgosi ke kgosi ka batho" that matched his view: "A chief is a chief, but only by the will of the people." He was volunteer-in-chief in the 1952 defiance campaign, which was formed to target the six worst discriminatory laws. But the government had become so repressive, Mandela found it hard to stick to just six laws. "Nelson was a key figure in thinking, planning and devising new tactics," Oliver Tambo would later say.

Ten thousand volunteers of all races decided to go to jail, often singing and dancing, by deliberately flouting unjust legislation in relays which were carefully choreographed to include alerting the baffled police of their intention to break the law. Those arrested, jailed and fined included Mandela, who was picked up by mistake on the evening of the first day of the campaign for breaking the night pass – the 11pm curfew for black South Africans who didn't have a special evening dispensation stamped in their hated pass books.

"I felt like explaining to him [the policeman] that I was in charge of running the campaign on a day-to-day basis and was not scheduled to defy and be arrested until much later, but of course that would have been ridiculous," Mandela said. "Until then I had spent bits and pieces of time in prison but this was my first concentrated experience." It would prepare him for longer stretches.

Government didn't listen to the voices of the passive resistance. A new law was passed so that people who protested against existing laws would be whipped and sentenced to hard labour. The angry state began to use taxpayers' money to insert spies into the ANC to watch Mandela and others. But the defiance campaign was in many ways a success that had alerted thousands of people to their own power; it also caught the eye of the international media, who, like the government, had noticed Mandela's easy charm and charisma. Unlike the government, the press did not think Mandela was a puppet or a communist pawn. But then, no elected government official had met face to face with Mandela.

Mandela continued to use legal means to fight back against apartheid – much to the distress of his white legal colleagues. In the 1950s, he very nearly lost the right to call himself a lawyer and appear in court because the provincial legal body, the Transvaal Law Society, objected to his leadership of the defiance campaign. How could a lawyer defy the laws, they indignantly petitioned the Supreme Court. But Mandela's view was clear: unjust laws are not meant to be obeyed.

Law was dry and dull and always on the defence, he noted. It didn't capture the imagination. So he was delighted when the ANC called in 1953 for a Congress of the People so that ordinary folk of all races and all political affiliations could express their views on how the country should be run.

Suggestions "came in from sports and cultural clubs, schools, trade union branches," Mandela said. "They came on serviettes, on paper torn from exercise books, on scraps of foolscap, on the backs of our own leaflets. It was humbling to see how the suggestions of ordinary people were often far ahead of those of the leaders. The most commonly cited demand was for one-man-one-vote."

He was also was very busy setting up what the

Members of the Movement for Colonial Freedom and the Black Sash (an organization for white women) unite to oppose government policy.

Walter Sisulu and Mandela share the news at the Johannesburg Supreme Court, during the defiance campaign.

Mandela's constant political activities were deeply upsetting for his wife Evelyn. While he was away campaigning, Evelyn suspected that he was actually visiting other women. This saddened her husband, but he would not compromise democracy for love. "She was a very good woman, charming, strong and faithful, and a fine mother," Mandela said. "I never lost my respect and admiration for her."

Shortly after the defiance campaign, Evelyn went south to the port city of Durban to become a midwife. Mandela's mother, Fanny, moved from her beloved Transkei to take care of his two boys while he was in courts and meetings, although he found a few moments to visit his wife on the east coast. On her return the couple had their second daughter, named after their first, who had died at such a young age: Makaziwe.

Mandela's other, far more political baby was the Congress of the People, which was two years in gestation and was eventually held in 1955 on a dusty, windswept patch of open ground in an old remnant of multiracial South Africa, Kliptown, some 40 kilometres south of "white" Johannesburg. Over two sunny days in the winter month of June, the gathering showed Mandela that a wide and disparate group of people – from earnest communists to cautious businessmen, whether Christian, Jew, Muslim, Hindu or atheist, white, black, coloured and Indian, male and female – could come together in pursuit of common goals. Mandela and his colleagues in the ANC had begun reaching out to allies of many shapes and sizes, something for which purists and fundamentalists would criticize them harshly in years to come. But this inclusive strategy opened a route, a path to unite an entire nation despite three hundred and fifty years of bitterness and grief. Not white or black but "The people shall rule!" predicted the Freedom Charter.

Mandela was then nearly 38, and under banning orders which barred him from speaking. He insisted on risking the drive to Kliptown to watch and learn at the edges of the crowd of 3000 delegates voting on the final draft. Security police milled around taking photographs and writing down names in notebooks while the crowd sang, listened to speeches, and voted.

ANC called the "Mandela Plan", or the "M Plan", which was meant to fight for democracy at street level even if organizations and high-ranking individuals were banned across the nation. Many people working in the struggle could see that increasingly aggressive policing and repression would bring an end to public campaigns. But Mandela thought that small groups of committed activists would be capable of carrying on work underground – a decision with far-reaching impact when the ANC was finally forced into answering violence with violence.

"THE PEOPLE SHALL RULE!"

The historic Freedom Charter, which begins with "South Africa belongs to all who live in it", was about to have its final vote when armed police rushed on to the platform and grabbed the microphone to accuse the audience of treason. Placards – including canteen signs for vegetarians warning: "Soup with meat" and "Soup without meat" – were torn down and confiscated.

The crowd did not fight back. They stood still, singing the haunting hymn "Nkosi sikelele iAfrika" – "God bless Africa, guide her people" – while one by one, police took down their details and let them go. Mandela safely disappeared through Kliptown's back routes, but there would be a long-running sequel to this moment.

In the meantime, the Freedom Charter which was born out of the Congress of the People did not go far enough for some. Mandela, once the youthful firebrand, suddenly found that he was not militant enough for some of his younger or angrier activist friends. The more extreme members of the ANC

June 1955, Kliptown. The Freedom Charter is created at the ANC's Congress of the People, representing and developing a set of principles for everybody in South Africa. One of those present was the Anglican Bishop Trevor Huddleston (left).

The historic Freedom Charter. Not white or black but "The people shall rule!" it predicted.

rejected the Freedom Charter and would soon break away to form the Pan Africanist Congress (PAC). This, ironically, was the group which was to capture the imagination of independence leaders across Africa, and indeed across much of the developing world, for many years to come. "Africa for Africans!" was their cry.

On the other hand, the Freedom Charter was too radical for others. A year after the Congress of the People, shortly before Christmas, the government had its revenge. Just after dawn, the security police bashed on the door of the Mandela home, frightening his wife and three small children. In front of his small son, Thembi, the police waved a warrant for his father's arrest.

The Afrikaans paperwork said he was being charged with *hoogverraad*. High treason. The punishment for treason: death. But Mandela was not alone. His legal partner, Oliver Tambo,

was also arrested. "The theatre of conflict is shifting to the law courts," Tambo calmly observed. He was correct.

In addition to the local activists, dozens of their colleagues from across the country were arrested and flown to Johannesburg, where they formed a sort of multiracial college of revolutionaries inside the prison cells for a few weeks while they waited to hear from the courts. But the prisoners, many of them isolated by banning orders, were delighted to meet each other. They even formed a choir. In total, 156 people involved in the creation of the Freedom Charter – almost the entire leadership of the ANC– were arrested for treason. The year was 1956. The trial would drag on until 1961.

Many attempts were made during the treason trial to dehumanize the prisoners. When he was transferred to "The Fort", as the hilltop Johannesburg prison was known, Mandela was

forced to strip naked and wait for more than an hour in the open air in the quadrangle, alongside a series of other shivering men. He was given only three thin blankets and a straw mat to sleep on. Evelyn dutifully visited – once. Vindictiveness by the state continued. Later the trial was shifted without explanation from Johannesburg to the Old Synagogue in the nearby city of Pretoria, causing the accused – by then out on bail – enormous transport costs and chewing up even more of their careers and personal life.

The treason trial began in Johannesburg's old Drill Hall, a military building selected because there were far too many accused to fit into a normal courtroom. Jubilant crowds and nervous policemen surrounded it but Mandela's wife Evelyn was not among the spectators. Always religious, after her return from Durban the newly qualified midwife became a Jehovah's Witness. The marriage

deteriorated into bitter fights over the children: she wanted them to distribute Watchtower pamphlets; he wanted them to hand out ANC leaflets. "When I would tell her that I was serving the nation, she would reply that serving God was above serving the nation," Mandela said. Evelyn had given her husband an ultimatum: abandon either the marriage or the African National Congress.

On the first day of the treason trial, an incompetent official forgot the microphones and loudspeakers, so nobody could hear the judge. On the second day the state introduced a new punishment. A vast wire cage had been created for the prisoners, which could seat well over 100 of them with just enough space for 16 armed guards as well. Their lawyers, however, were not allowed to enter the cage for their usual consultations and were furious at this clumsy behaviour in a courtroom. The accused, meanwhile, did not lose

Members of the Black Sash hold a candlelit vigil.

The accused in the defiance campaign, which was formed to target the six worst discriminatory laws. But the government had become so repressive, Mandela found it hard to stick to just six laws. His view was clear: unjust laws are not meant to be obeyed.

their sense of humour. One of them promptly pinned a handwritten sign to the diamond-shaped mesh: "Dangerous animals! Do not feed!" The defence team had to threaten to stage a court walkout before the cage was dismantled. A few days later, Mandela was freed on bail, although he had to report to the police once a week and was not allowed to attend public gatherings.

When Mandela received bail, he returned to an empty house for the Christmas summer holidays. Evelyn had given up. She stripped the tiny house of everything, including curtains, and moved out, taking the children with her. But she hadn't left Johannesburg. She had moved in with her brother and so Mandela was able to retain some links with his children.

The treason trial was larger than life. It took two days for the chief prosecutor to read the charges. It took much of 1957 simply to list the 12,000 pieces of state evidence, which included the two signs grabbed from the food queue at the Congress of the People: "Soup with meat" and "Soup without meat". Mandela often brought a book to read, or worked on a legal brief.

A University of Cape Town expert testifying for the state made a fool of himself when he confidently described a paragraph of evidence as "communism straight from the shoulder". He had written it himself. The garbled testimony from the policemen revealed that many of the detectives who had been spying at the Congress of the People in Kliptown did not understand English. At one point the

Mandela leaves court in Pretoria. "The proceedings are not as funny as they may seem," the magistrate warned the accused.

The actual trial would only take place in August 1959, more than two-and-a-half years after the arrests in the middle of the night. All but ten of the 210 witnesses called by the state would be policemen. As one of Mandela's Fort Hare university professors, the brilliant Z. K. Matthews, once noted, it was the police who formed "the main link between the African people and the government". They would prove to be an untrustworthy link.

The treason trial dragged on for four years. In law courts across the country, the minority government was trying to use legal means to stifle all kinds of voices of dissent. Hundreds of black women who protested against being forced to carry the passes, now renamed reference books, were on trial. Other people were charged with incitement, merely for advocating stayaways during the 1958 whites-only election. Hundreds of subsistence farmers faced murder charges during the uprising against corrupt chiefs in Sekhukhuneland in the north.

It is no wonder that more militant minds formed the PAC during the treason trial. After all, they argued, the moderate strategies adopted by Mandela and others had failed to stop the night-time terror in the densely populated multiracial suburb of Sophiatown, when Johannesburg police with guns forced owners and tenants from their homes, which were then bulldozed and reincarnated as a whites-only suburb with the gloating new name of *Triomf*, or triumph. Mandela's first banning order had expired when he threw himself into the campaign against forced removals in western Johannesburg, and he was promptly banned for the second time. In the meantime, the government engineered utterly segregated cities and towns with the notorious Group Areas Act.

Nor had Mandela been able to block the imposition of mediocre Bantu Education on black students, which brought an end to the high standards of many of the mission schools. "When I have control of native education," said the architect of the legislation, who was inspired by Nazi ideas of purity, "I will reform it so that natives will be taught from childhood to realize that equality with Europeans is not for them. There is no place for him

magistrate had to scold the laughing treason trialists: "The proceedings are not as funny as they may seem," he warned.

After a year on trial, charges were dropped without warning or explanation against 61 of the 156 accused. Mandela's law partner, Tambo, was freed, which was good news for their struggling legal practice. Mandela himself remained one of the accused. In 1959, another 65 treason trialists were let go. Only 30 of the original intake of 153 were left facing high treason. They included Mandela. Clearly, he was a marked man.

"I never expected justice in court, however much I fought for it, and though I sometimes received it," Mandela commented years later.

"THE PEOPLE SHALL RULE!"

Sophiatown: a shantytown for black South Africans. From 1955 Johannesburg police with guns forced owners and tenants from their homes, which were then bulldozed and reincarnated as a whites-only suburb with the gloating new name of *Triomf*, or triumph.

in European society above the level of certain forms of labour. What is the use of teaching a Bantu child mathematics when it cannot use it in practice?"

At the same time, it was a slightly bizarre era of courtesy between foes. During the treason trial, when Mandela was detained without trial during the first state of emergency, a police colonel permitted him to travel from Pretoria Central Jail to Johannesburg at weekends to wind up the legal offices of Mandela and Tambo. Mandela would be accompanied from court every Friday afternoon by a single sergeant, who would buy *biltong* (dried chewy sticks of meat), oranges and chocolate for them both, accompany him to the local police station to be locked up on Friday, Saturday and Sunday nights, and then drive him back to court on Monday morning.

This brief, civilized peace between opponents was not to last. "During the treason trial, there were no examples of individuals being isolated, beaten and tortured in order to elicit information," Mandela wrote. "All of those things became commonplace thereafter."

One day during a break in the endless, monotonous treason trial sessions, Mandela was giving a neighbour a lift to the medical school. They went past the landmark Baragwanath Teaching Hospital, one of the few places which treated black patients. For some reason, Mandela glanced at the bus stop queue.

"I noticed out of the corner of my eye a lovely young woman," he said. Always impetuous, Mandela instantly wanted a better look but the heavy flow of traffic was unstoppable. The mystery face lingered

Mandela lets off some steam. Boxing and soccer were virtually the only sports allowed in the township.

in his imagination. Or at least, that's one version of the story. The lady in question had already glimpsed the lawyer in action in court one day.

According to Mandela, one day he entered Oliver Tambo's office to find the same wide-eyed young woman from the bus stop, now sitting there with her brother on a legal matter. He was surprised, but the truth was that almost all of black Johannesburg ended up at the Mandela and Tambo firm sooner or later, in trouble with the new laws.

"This is Nomzamo (one who undergoes trials)," Tambo said politely. It turned out that the stunning Nomzamo Winifred Madikizela came from an area not far away from the Mandela homestead, one of the 11 children of a businessman and his wife. She had been waiting at the Bara bus rank because she too was a trailbreaker: the hospital's first black social worker.

Mandela's head was buzzing. "Something in me was deeply stirred by her presence," he confessed later. "I was thinking more of how I could ask her out than how our firm would handle her case."

Mandela was bewitched. "I cannot say for certain if there is such a thing as love at first sight," he wrote as an elderly man. "But I do know that the moment I glimpsed Winnie Nomzamo, I knew that I wanted her as my wife."

The impulsive young lawyer wasted no time. Within a day he phoned the much younger woman at her work with some made-up nonsense about needing her help to raise funds to pay for the treason trial lawyers. He took Winnie back into town to lunch at one of the few restaurants that served blacks, where she had her first spicy curry, diluted with many glasses of water.

By the end of the day, he proposed. "I knew at once that I wanted to marry her – and I told her so. Her spirit, her passion, her youth, her courage, her wilfulness – I felt all of these things the moment I first saw her."

It was an unusual engagement. In the evening, the shy woman would watch as her boyfriend worked out his stresses in evening boxing sessions at the gym. Afterwards, she might sit in the audience as Mandela, although officially banned, continued his lobbying activities at ANC gatherings. He read thick books. She read fashion magazines.

> "During the treason trial, there were no examples of individuals being isolated, beaten and tortured in order to elicit information," Mandela wrote. "All of those things became commonplace thereafter."

During the day, if she wasn't working, Winnie might squeeze in a brief meeting at the struggling law offices or attend treason trial sessions in the cavernous old Drill Hall. She couldn't talk to her fiancée in the dock, but her presence was electrifying.

"Though I was on trial for treason, Winnie gave me cause for hope," Mandela said. "I felt as though I had a new and second chance at life. My love for her gave me added strength."

Mandela was not just asking Winnie to be his wife. He was able to pay the usual *lobola*, or bride-price, once the family had reluctantly come to accept the match, but *lobola* was where traditional roles ended – Mandela was asking Winnie to support him financially on her tiny salary. The treason trial was destroying his law practice but he could not give up on the struggle for freedom.

And he had learnt something from the breakdown of his first marriage. Sitting in at political meetings had been a deliberate test: Winnie had to support him politically. Often this meant not knowing where he was, or what he was doing, until he returned home late at night.

"The wife of a freedom fighter is often like a widow, even when her husband is not in prison," Mandela noted.

In order to marry at the Madikizela ancestral home in the Transkei, Mandela had to beg the authorities for a temporary alteration to his banning orders so he could travel outside Johannesburg. Only six days were allowed, which gave just enough time to drive down, marry and return without the usual formalities of introducing the bride to her husband's ancestral home.

Winnie's father, a former school principal, spoke surprisingly sombre words at the 1958 wedding reception. He was not optimistic about the future, he said. Such a marriage would face many unending tests. "You are marrying a man who is already married to the struggle," Columbus Madikizela warned his beautiful daughter, who had never had to worry about where her next meal came from, even if she had never worn shoes until high school. He ended with a phrase which advocates wives standing by their husbands under any circumstances: "If your man is a wizard, you must become a witch!"

He did not know how accurate his words would turn out to be.

The new couple never had a honeymoon. Instead,

June 1958. "I cannot say for certain if there is such a thing as love at first sight, but I do know that the moment I glimpsed Winnie Nomzamo, I knew that I wanted her as my wife."

Women protesting against the Pass Laws in the 1950s. New laws, extending the restrictive passes, made women criminals in their own country, liable to arrest and jail for walking to buy a loaf of bread.

they would wake up at four in the morning in his tiny house in Orlando West, the same home he had shared with Evelyn and their children until the marriage broke up. Winnie would light the coal stove and prepare breakfast. Together, they would get ready for another day of constantly juggling treason trial appearances, work and politics.

Almost immediately, Winnie proved to be as fiery as her much older husband. She informed him one evening that she intended to join the many women protesting against new laws extending the restrictive internal passports, or passes. The passes made women criminals in their own country, liable to arrest and jail for walking to a store to buy a loaf of bread.

Mandela found himself in the odd position of warning her against the protest. She would certainly be arrested. Then she would certainly be fired – and it was her small salary that was supporting the family. After that, she would be blacklisted and nobody would hire her. In addition, she was pregnant with their first child. The next day, Winnie Mandela went to Johannesburg's central pass office with hundreds of other women and was duly arrested by armed policemen.

Mandela and Tambo was the law firm of choice for most of the arrested women. When Winnie saw her husband, in the Marshall Square police station, she "beamed" as though "she had given me a great gift that she knew would please me". But Mandela only had time to say how proud he was of her, because soon 2000 local women had been arrested – and the authorities were running out of blankets, mats, toilets and food. Winnie was freed on bail within two weeks.

In February 1959, Mandela returned home after midnight to find his heavily pregnant wife alone and in pain. He rushed Winnie to her original place of work at Baragwanath Hospital, but could not stay. He had to attend the treason trial hearings in Pretoria.

On his return, he was introduced to their new daughter, Zenani. The poetic name can be translated as a challenge, along the lines of, "What have you brought to the world?" Once more, Mandela's elderly mother came up from the Transkei to assist her newest daughter-in-law or *makoti*.

Winnie Mandela, new mother, trail-blazing social worker and now a jailbird like her husband, was just 25. "I never promised her gold and diamonds," Mandela said, perhaps a tad wistfully. "And I was never able to give them to her."

STRAND EN SEE
NET BLANKES

BEACH AND SEA
WHITES ONLY

⟵⟶

CHAPTER 4

The Winds of Change
Blow – Backwards

The 1960s began in hope for Nelson Mandela. While other African countries had celebrated their independence already – Ghana was the first, three years earlier – there was never another year like 1960 for political freedom across the continent. Seventeen African colonies attained independence this year, giving him renewed hope. Moreover, on a personal level, his second daughter from his second marriage, Zindziswa, was born, giving him great happiness even though he could spend only brief moments with her.

In 1961, he would even be acquitted in the treason trial and could speak in public for the first time in years, as the police forgot to renew his expired banning orders. Yet by the end of the same year, Nelson Mandela would be on the run, his organization banned, his career in tatters, any hopes of peaceful change evaporated – and worse to come as the decade progressed.

In February 1960, British Prime Minister Harold Macmillan stood before the whites-only parliament in Cape Town and warned the sneering politicians of the "winds of change" blowing through Africa. Within weeks, events would prove Macmillan right – and wrong. "The winds of change had indeed blown in South Africa," wrote author Elinor Sisulu. "But they had blown backwards."

On the morning of March 21, while Nelson Mandela was being collected by the rickety treason bus to attend the daily treason trial hearings, police throughout South Africa were preparing for unarmed protestors from rival organization, the Pan Africanist Congress, who criticized Mandela and his colleagues for not fighting hard enough for people's freedom. The PAC believed in direct confrontation, not time-consuming negotiations, and they were bitterly suspicious of Mandela and his comrades for working with people of other races and viewpoints.

As he boarded the bus, Mandela saw some of the PAC leaders, his former colleagues, walk towards the police station to show the police that they were not carrying the hated pass book – ready to insist that they should be arrested and not given bail. Mandela was dubious about the benefit of this campaign, which he thought was badly organized and put the lives of people at risk unnecessarily.

Events would prove him right – but not in Johannesburg. The pivotal event happened 60 kilometres south-west in the grimy industrial town of Vereeniging, which once had a reputation for peacefulness simply because the treaty ending the last Anglo-Boer War was signed there nearly six decades earlier. It happened in a dormitory township for its poorly paid, badly housed black workers, called Sharpeville, where unarmed protestors had gathered to burn their passes and court arrest. Instead, they found death.

Many South African newspaper reports claimed that the crowd had stoned the police before the police opened fire, but one of the most trustworthy accounts comes from a Humphrey Tyler, then assistant editor of the influential *Drum* magazine. Tyler's words are worth using in full:

"As we drove through the fringes of the township many people shouted the Pan-Africanist slogan 'Izwe Lethu', which means 'Our Land', or gave the thumbs-up 'freedom' salute and shouted 'Afrika!'. They were grinning, cheerful, and nobody seemed

Apartheid beaches in Johannesburg with luxury apartments in the background. Any non-white found on the beach or in the sea would be prosecuted.

A haunting image of the Sharpeville massacre, which was to draw international attention to and condemnation of the South African government. A South African cabinet minister later dismissed Sharpeville as "an ordinary police action".

"... how could black and white ever live together again in peace and harmony?"

to be afraid ... There were crowds in the streets as we approached the police station. There were plenty of police, too, wearing more guns and ammunition than uniforms ... The local Pan-Africanist leader ... told [us] his organization was against violence and that the crowd was there for a peaceful demonstration ... The crowd seemed perfectly amiable. It certainly never crossed our minds that they would attack us or anybody ...

There were sudden shrill cries of 'Izwe Lethu' from near the police, and I could see a small section of the crowd swirl around the Saracens [British-built armoured personnel carriers] and hands went up in the Africanist salute. Then the shooting started. We heard the chatter of a machine gun, then another, then another. There were hundreds of women, some of them laughing. They must have thought the police were firing blanks. One woman was hit about ten yards from our car. Her companion, a young man, went back when she fell. He thought she had stumbled. Then he turned her over and saw that her chest had been shot away. He looked at the blood on his hand and said: 'My God, she's gone!' Hundreds of kids were running, too.

One little boy had on an old blanket coat, which he held up behind his head, thinking, perhaps, that it might save him from the bullets. Some of the children, hardly as tall as the grass, were leaping like rabbits. Some were shot, too. Still the shooting went on. One of the policemen was standing on top of a Saracen, and it looked as though he was firing his gun into the crowd. He was swinging it around in a wide arc from his hip as though he were panning a movie camera. Two other officers were with him, and it looked as if they were firing pistols ... One man, who had been lying still, dazedly got to his feet, staggered a few yards, then fell in a heap. A woman sat with her head cupped in her hands.

One by one the guns stopped.

Before the shooting, I heard no warning to the crowd to disperse. There was no warning volley. When the shooting started it did not stop until there was no living thing in the huge compound in front of the police station. The police have claimed they were in desperate danger because the crowd was stoning them. Yet only three policemen were reported to have been hit by stones – and more than 200 Africans were shot down. The police also have said that the crowd was armed with 'ferocious weapons', which littered the compound after they fled.

I saw no weapons, although I looked very carefully, and afterwards studied the photographs of the death scene. While I was there I saw only shoes, hats and a few bicycles left among the bodies. The crowd gave me no reason to feel scared, though I moved among them without any distinguishing mark to protect me, quite obvious with my white skin."

Sixty-nine people died, most of them shot in the back. Another 186 were wounded, many severely. Again, almost all of them were shot in the back. The wounded, taken to hospital, were then placed under arrest. Among the dead and the hurt, many were women and children. Three policemen reported being hit with stones; none was hurt badly enough to require medical attention.

Sharpeville was not South Africa's first massacre. People still remembered what happened forty years earlier in remote Bulhoek, in a region not far away from the Mandela family homestead, in the midst of the religious frenzy to convert Africans from traditional ancestor worship to Christianity.

That was when more than 1000 heavily armed police shot dead more than 150 peasants, wounding more and jailing as many survivors as they could find. But back in the 1920s, news of the Bulhoek massacre did not flash across the world. In the 1960s, with higher literacy rates, radio commonplace and television growing in the outside world, the impact of the Sharpeville massacre – especially the photographs of the corpses – was enormous. Abroad, the American government, facing its own struggle for human rights for the descendants of slaves stolen from

Africa, scolded South Africa's white government. The United Nations condemned the event, the slow start to a worldwide decades-long campaign to isolate apartheid. But a South African cabinet minister later dismissed Sharpeville as "an ordinary police action".

"How many more Sharpevilles could the country stand without violence and terror becoming the order of the day?" Mandela would demand in court. "And if this happened, how could black and white ever live together again in peace and harmony?"

Closer to home, other African countries remembered with sorrow their own colonial-era massacres, and resolved that when the time came, they would offer as much financial and military support for the fight for freedom in South Africa as possible. Many of the former British colonies began a campaign, which was successful a year later, to expel South Africa from the Commonwealth. However, offers of assistance from the newly independent African countries would be a mixed blessing for Nelson Mandela. When he later slipped out of the country to lobby freshly minted African governments for help, they had all heard of Sharpeville – and wanted to give money to the militant PAC organizers, not to his organization. "Africa for Africans" – the PAC slogan – had captured their imagination. Mandela was frequently advised to give up on the ANC, or get his colleagues to merge with the PAC. Mandela would refuse to give up on his multiracial and multicultural ideals.

But that was still in the future. Immediately after the Sharpeville massacre, the Johannesburg stock market quavered and housing markets collapsed as white South Africans responded to the newspaper

The bulldozed Sophiatown ready to make way for a new white suburb. Ironically, the Sharpeville massacre would cause an exodus of white citizens from South Africa, leading housing markets to collapse.

Outside the courtroom nothing changes: benches for non-whites in a Johannesburg municipal park.

pictures. Some were convinced of an imminent revenge attack, or that nothing they could do could help push the government towards negotiation, and fled the country. News of the Sharpeville massacre even trickled into the treason trial courtroom in Pretoria as Mandela sat, watching his respected leader Chief Albert Luthuli, president-general of the ANC, give evidence.

Later, Luthuli marvelled at "how easy it would have been in South Africa for the natural feelings of resentment at white domination to have been turned into feelings of hatred and a desire for revenge against the white community" after Sharpeville.

"It could well be expected that a racialism equal to that of their oppressors would flourish to counter the white arrogance towards blacks," he noted. He confidently predicted that this interracial warfare would never happen because the ANC leadership "had set itself steadfastly against racial vain-gloriousness." Decades after Luthuli's mysterious death at a railway crossing while he was under house arrest, Nelson Mandela would say something very similar in his first pronouncements as a free man.

That night, depressed and disturbed, while much of the country mourned, Mandela met with fellow political activists, white and black, to work out an appropriate response to the tragedy. They decided to call for a national day of mourning on the next Monday. But many people thought that a stayaway was a pathetic reaction. They called for blood to be met with blood. "Patience," counselled Mandela.

In response to the news of the stay-at-home strike, a day before it started, the government suddenly relaxed the hated pass laws. If the relaxation of the pass laws was meant to convince people not to participate in the strike, it was an abysmal failure. The day of mourning turned out to be the biggest stay-at-home strike in South African history. Factories across the country had to switch off their machines and wait. Madams had to clean their own clothes. Office staff found themselves stumbling around the sugar and china cups at tea break.

Photographs show that Mandela, smiling broadly, was among those who then burnt his despised pass book without going to jail, taking advantage of this unexpected moment when black South Africans were not treated as strangers in their own land. But he knew that this temporary truce was not a sign that the government was committed to change, but was more likely just to give it breathing space to ready its own forces for a counterattack. He was correct. The next important announcement was not an apology for the massacre or the creation of an enquiry into police behaviour. Instead, on the day of mourning itself, as if to rub salt into the wounds of the survivors, the government announced a piece of legislation: the Unlawful Organisations Bill. It had already banned the Communist Party, now, the government was going to ban not only the Pan Africanist Congress but the African National Congress as well.

The government minister who announced that the pass laws would be abolished was sent into diplomatic purgatory in Latin America. The Christian bastion of apartheid, the Dutch Reformed Church, which had briefly condemned the pass laws, was summoned before the Prime Minister for a resounding scolding. White unity was paramount.

Mandela had to say a sad goodbye to Oliver Tambo. They had already agreed that if the government was going to consider banning the organization, it was important that a senior activist should leave the country to keep the fight for freedom continuing on the outside. Tambo had already been dropped as one of the treason trial accused, so his disappearance would not be as noticeable.

The lawyer had long been planning to follow his heart's urging to become a minister but recognized with resignation that his ambassadorial skills would come in useful. A Cape Town-based journalist agreed to borrow his mother's car and the day after the stay-at-home strike in memory of the massacre, they readied themselves for the three-hour drive from Johannesburg north into what is now Botswana. As a British protectorate, then called Bechuanaland, it did not require passports from former British colony South Africa.

Safely driving over the border to the small town of Lobatse, Oliver Tambo found not freedom but a familiar scenario. The hotel allowed only white guests, so he had to stay at a hostel a few miles outside of town. No restaurant would serve them,

The International Olympic Committee barred South Africa from the 1964 Olympic Games in Tokyo, unless the government renounced racial discrimination in sport and opposed the ban on competition between white and black athletes. It did not.

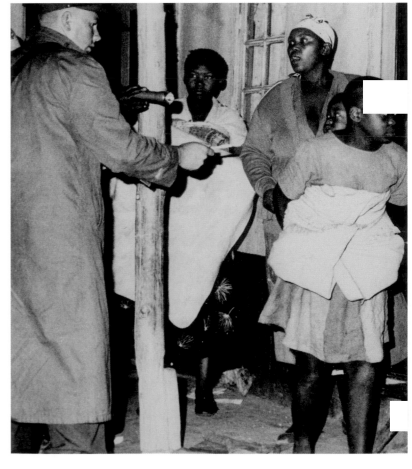

Cato Manor, Durban. Police rouse black South Africans from their sleep and take them in for questioning.

so they bought biscuits and fruit. Almost immediately, the South African government sent two security officers over the border to abduct him, but they gave the game away by discussing their plans in Afrikaans over a cold beer in a bar, thinking nobody would understand them. Another journalist, enjoying his own beer, passed on a warning. An old school friend was persuaded by the state to try to kidnap him, armed with a mask and chloroform. Both attempts failed, and Tambo made his way to Tanganyika in a

> "Blankets were encrusted with dried blood, ridden with lice, vermin and cockroaches, and reeked with a stench that actually competed with the stink of the drain."

small chartered plane. Oliver Tambo, without money or even a passport, would not be allowed home for more than three decades. While in exile, this quiet, persistent, methodical man did more than anyone else to keep the memory of Nelson Mandela alive.

Tambo left just in time. Some 24 hours later, Nelson Mandela was arrested. Even though he was already on trial, and could have been collected at the courtroom, half-a-dozen armed security policemen smashed his front door at 1am. His wife, although they did not know it yet, was pregnant with their second child. But when Mandela reached his police cell in western Johannesburg, he found that he was in good company – so much good company that the prisoners had to stand; there were too many to sit.

Government forces, shouting and screaming, thumped and bashed on the doors of virtually every known activist in the country – even some older people who had dropped out of politics years earlier. Nearly two thousand people were arrested. In several cases affecting families, both the father and the mother were taken to jail; 19 children were stranded. When the children held up placards

protesting at their parents' arrest on the steps of the Johannesburg city hall, the children too were arrested and held at a police station for several hours.

By evening the hungry, tired huddle of prisoners had been allowed one communal meal of watery cornmeal porridge, without utensils, and given specially selected bedding: "Blankets were encrusted with dried blood, ridden with lice, vermin and cockroaches, and reeked with a stench that actually competed with the stink of the drain," Mandela wrote. The toilet drain in the corner of the bare concrete floor, he explained, was blocked.

Close to midnight, each activist was called individually to the front yard of the police station. When it was Mandela's turn, he was told he was free to go by the grinning police officers. Then they arrested him again before he could move. The state of emergency regulations just imposed by the frightened government had erased even the limited legal rights available before. This was martial law. Mandela could be arrested, released and re-arrested without even being accused of a crime. He would remain incarcerated for five months, without ever being charged with a crime. This was the government's response to the ANC's Freedom Charter, which said, "South Africa belongs to all who live in it". No, said the government: it belongs to us.

Meanwhile, oddly enough, other events continued as if the terrifying new legislation had made no difference. The treason trial judges objected to having an empty witness box after virtually all the accused were detained without trial in police cells across the region, so those particular activists, including Mandela, were moved to a Pretoria jail, from which they shuttled back and forth from the trial under police guard. The treason trial entered its 100th day, which Mandela and the other activists cheerfully marked with slices of delicious cake, as if it were a birthday party. They knew that the punishment for high treason was death but the activists insisted on behaving as if the state itself was in the dock.

All this time, the monotonous treason trial had been devoted to the prosecution. Now was meant to be the moment for defence to shine. But Mandela argued that it was now impossible for their people to

testify for the defence, when the ANC was banned, the accused had been detained without trial and the new emergency regulations might forbid even courtroom testimony. The judge agreed, despite objections from the prosecution, and the court case took a short break.

All the activists, black and white, were held in a vermin-infested, stifling, overcrowded prison in Pretoria, the civil service capital of the country, over the Easter religious holiday break – although the white prisoners had better medical treatment, better food, more space and slightly fewer bugs. "Our white men's prison palace" was how a fellow lawyer-prisoner-activist, Joe Slovo, laughingly described it.

Low-ranking prison warders seemed to enjoy using the new emergency regulations to harass Mandela and the others. Their lawyers would drive all the way from Johannesburg, the city of business, to Pretoria, one of the three centres of government in the country, and then be told to wait patiently. After greeting their clients, the lawyers were

Lilian Ngoyi (centre left) was once thought of as the ideal wife for Mandela. She's seen here with Amina Cachalia, Helen Joseph and Sophy Williams leading a famous women's protest.

Mandela's friend Helen Suzman died on New Year's Day 2009, aged 91. She visited Mandela in prison many times. While they didn't always agree, she always helped him in practical ways – such as removing a swastika-wearing prison guard.

NELSON MANDELA

then told after a few minutes by gloating guards that their time was up. Mandela and the others would be returned to their cold cells. The rule of law was eroding.

While in prison, Mandela came to the difficult conclusion that there was no point in lawyers representing him – or any of the accused activists – while the rule of law was suspended under the State of Emergency. The lawyer was fast losing hope in the law. As a result, when the treason trialists returned to the court, they shocked the judge by announcing that they were firing their lawyers. Only two of the accused, they said, would represent the trialists. One was Duma Nokwe, the first African advocate in the vast Transvaal province's supreme court, even though a government order barred him from taking chambers with his white colleagues near the courts and ordered him to find an office in a remote African township. The other man who would represent the treason trialists was Nelson Mandela.

The duo of Nokwe and Mandela hatched a creative plan to drag the trial out until this strange new bureaucratic nightmare, the state of emergency, had ended and their usual legal team could return: a plan which was sure to irritate and frustrate the prosecution. There were fewer than thirty accused left out of the original intake of 153 men and women. Each of the accused was asked by Mandela and Nokwe to cross-examine all of the rest of their fellow accused – so each person would repeat the same questions to more than two dozen men and women. This carried on until the state of emergency was lifted on the last day of August and their highly skilled defence lawyers returned for the last stages of the trial.

Mandela managed to achieve some small victories during the state of emergency. After long negotiations all the accused were allowed to meet with each other for group consultations. But this went against government regulations forbidding the mixing of prisoners of different sexes, so the prison created a complicated system of iron grills and partitions. This ensured that the black female treason trialists such as the noted former nurse Lillian Ngoyi, known as "the mother of black resistance", or Bertha Mashaba, a trade unionist

The treason trial choir. Mandela and co-defendants sing outside the Drill Hall. Winnie stands behind.

Happier times with family – a much older Mandela and his grandson, Bambatha, in 1990. "I love playing with children and chatting with them; it has always been one of the things that makes me feel most at peace."

who was one of the first people to be arrested during the defiance campaign, did not consort with men they had worked with for years. They were kept like animals in a zoo – and dangerous animals, at that.

More important was the fact that none of the black prisoners were supposed to be in contact with anyone across the race barrier, prisoners included. So even though Lillian Ngoyi had marched at the head of a vast column of 20,000 women with her co-accused friend Helen Joseph in the 1956 protest against imposing the pass laws on African women, they had to sit in separate cages. Helen was white.

In the same way, a white activist, such as Leon Levy, the trade unionist who became the first person in the country to be jailed without trial for the full 90-day limit, was separated in his own cage only for whites. "Even a master architect would have had trouble designing such a structure," Mandela commented later. The situation was ridiculous because the prisoners were allowed to mingle with each other in the court room. Such petty insults simply made the prisoners more determined. They

dismantled the barriers – and the prison authorities suddenly found it prudent to look the other way. Despite this small victory, Mandela and the others found themselves stuck in prison as the southern hemisphere underwent winter: March, April, May, June, July and August.

During this time, the prisoners held discussions about the possibility of armed struggle. As his close friend Walter Sisulu remembered it: "Some people felt that since they were in jail anyway, for non-violent protest, they might as well go to prison for something more tangible." This was a slowly ripening fruit; the time was not yet right to pluck it. Anyhow, Mandela was a lawyer – how could he learn to be a soldier? The idea of cooking up an armed uprising in the most non-violent way possible began to occupy his mind.

Outside prison, the whites-only government – still fighting the ghosts of the Anglo-Boer war of half a century ago – had announced that it would hold a referendum to gauge voters' mood on whether South Africa should break its historical ties with Britain and become a republic. The referendum, for white voters only, was held in October 1960, while

the final witness for the defence in the treason trial was telling the prosecutor that African people prized freedom above all else. A narrow majority of white voters voted in favour of going it alone, and a date was set for the creation of the new republic: May 31, 1961. This was not good news for the activists. The government had responded to international criticism by turning its back on the world.

After the state of emergency regulations were lifted, Mandela was allowed out of prison, and could embrace his pregnant wife for the first time in five months. He worked as a lawyer from the living room of a young Indian friend's flat in Johannesburg and dutifully showed up for his treason trial appearances, where the judges were by now openly irritated with the prosecutor's clumsy mistakes in his month-long summing up of the case. But Mandela's focus was on the reluctant transformation of the continent's oldest liberation movement from an open, transparent, democratic institution to a creature of the shadows. The South African Government had declared war upon its own people. The ANC would have no option but to go

underground. And its key leader would be Nelson Mandela.

Juggling repression, family, work and the treason trial proved exhausting. Mandela even secretly violated his banning orders confining him to Johannesburg during the treason trial's Christmas adjournment after discovering that his son, Makgatho, was seriously ill in the rural Transkei. Mandela drove through the night and ferried his son back to Johannesburg for urgent surgery, returning just in time to find that Winnie had given birth to another baby girl on her own. A lover of both poetry and irony, Mandela named the newborn after the daughter of a renowned Xhosa poet who had also been separated from his pregnant wife.

"Zindziswa", or "You are well-established", would be his last child. If not sentenced to jail in the treason trial, Mandela was planning to go underground to avoid the constant, paralyzing attentions of the enemy. Winnie knew. Her stoical response was to pack a suitcase and not ask questions her husband couldn't answer. Either way, her girls were going to lose their father: the courts would swallow him up, or the struggle for freedom would.

CHAPTER 5

The Attack of the Wild Beast

The treason trial was abruptly adjourned for a week in March 1961. It seemed likely that the judges had decided that the trial had dragged on long enough, and they were about to announce their final decision. A delighted Mandela recognized a golden opportunity. In their zeal the authorities forgot one important piece of paperwork. The bans they had served on Mandela were about to expire – but he was not going to remind them of their own mistake.

It was his first chance in five years to speak in public. He secretly drove 300 miles south to the capital of the then province of Natal to address one of the front organizations which had sprung up in the wake of the banning of the ANC. He used his precious free time in Pietermaritzburg to call on the government to hold a national convention involving all the relevant parties to design a democratic and multiracial constitution. If not, the government could expect nationwide demonstrations to drown out any celebrations of the new, internationally isolated republic. The government – more interested in avenging itself for past defeats by the British than considering South Africa's future – described Mandela as "arrogant" and ignored his call. He would barely be glimpsed in public again for a long time.

Mandela returned to Johannesburg, and on Monday he and all the remaining treason trialists were acquitted in neighbouring Pretoria. But their smiles were forced. "It was ironic that the court had come to the conclusion that non-violence was the policy of the ANC at the very same time that the ANC leadership was questioning its effectiveness," notes Elinor Sisulu, daughter-in-law of Walter Sisulu.

The activists knew that the state would find the verdict deeply, excruciatingly humiliating. Mandela's assessment was brutally simple. Within the legal system, the government was likely to pack the ranks of judges with its own obedient supporters. And it was quite likely that it would simply bypass the courtrooms and lawyers entirely, preferring more immediate vigilante-style justice. The era of routine beatings, torture and rape was coming closer and closer. He did not sleep at home that night – or for many nights to come.

The loneliness of living on the run hurt Nelson Mandela psychologically. "One has to plan every action, however small and seemingly insignificant," he recalled years later. "Nothing is innocent. Everything is questioned. You cannot be yourself."

In many ways, the government had inadvertently prepared Mandela for this life: he had been living almost on the run already, ducking and diving from banning restrictions and the unwanted attentions of policemen for over a decade. Even when the ANC was banned, Mandela didn't cave in. He simply remodelled his lifestyle. From being an early-morning riser, he became a creature of the night. He slept in the spare bedrooms or on the sofas of a series of homes and flats lent by sympathizers, reliant on them for food and drink and necessities. He stayed in during the day and moved around the country only at night, even though he risked arrest for not having the correct night pass. He slept badly.

Often, he seems to have been saved as much by the astonishing stupidity of the apartheid state – convinced by its own propaganda about the backwardness of its black citizens – as by his own

In October 1958, several hundred black women who had protested against the pass laws appeared before Johannesburg magistrates accused of disturbing the peace. Outside the courtroom, police cleared the streets of black demonstrators using batons, canes, handcuffs and tear-gas.

Liliesleaf Farm in the 1960s. Mandela worked at the farm, a safe house, as a cook and waiter.

skill at becoming invisible. He took terrible risks. The police, who issued a warrant of arrest for him, distributed a picture of him with a beard. Friends urged him to shave off his facial hair. Mandela refused. He had become too attached to it. Sometimes, the authorities gained an idea of his itinerary because he took to phoning newspapers from public telephone boxes to poke fun at the police and promote the struggle. "What are you going to do?" he asked in a letter sent from the underground to the newspapers. "Are you going to remain silent and neutral in a matter of life and death to my people, to our people? For my own part I have made my choice. I will not leave South Africa, nor will I surrender."

Mandela's disguises were humble. They had to be. Bearded, scruffy, in blue overalls, he was an anonymous, almost invisible garden boy – a widely used demeaning term for an adult, which was one

of the terms he specifically condemned and personally outlawed in his first speech to parliament decades later.

In another disguise, he was the cook for workers on a renovation job at the Liliesleaf Farm in Rivonia, north of Johannesburg, which had been bought as a safe house. Sometimes his children from both marriages would visit. Only at night did his real work take over.

In one incident at the farm, he got irritated with waiting for a man who was telling a long story. "In mild exasperation, I started to move away," Mandela recounts in his autobiography. "At that point he noticed me and said sharply, 'Waiter, come back here, I didn't say you could leave.'"

Mandela's own sense of dignity had imperilled him. Like many, he had to fake a happy servitude in order to survive. "To those men, I was an inferior, a servant, a person without a trade and therefore to

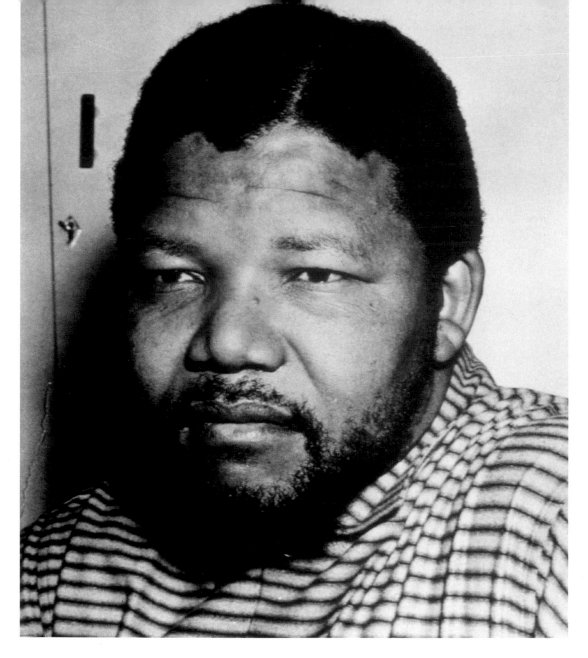

On the run. Mandela refused to shave off his beard despite police photos showing him wearing one. He had become attached to it.

be treated with disdain. I played the role so well that none of them suspected I was anything other." It was a difficult role to play for an esteemed lawyer who was fighting for the dignity of black people.

In Cape Town, a prayer by a township minister during his time underground struck a resounding chord in his mind. "Lord, some of your subjects are more downtrodden than others. Are you not paying attention?" After which the minister issued a veiled warning: if the Lord did not use a little more initiative in leading the black man to salvation, the black man would have to take matters into his own two hands. "Amen," said Mandela.

The outlaw also discovered that life underground wasn't that different in many respects from ordinary life as a black person in what was intended by the authorities to be a white man's country. There were so many regulations that even the most careful and scrupulous black citizens ended up in constant

trouble with the law – in fact, for many people, jail lost its stigma because they were thrown into it so often.

The Republic Day protests were an astonishing sight. It's hard to imagine that a stay-at-home could trigger such a response: mass arrests, helicopters hovering over townships, armoured tanks on patrol, the largest military call-up of able-bodied white men since World War II, public holidays cancelled, police and soldiers everywhere.

The English-language press, considered more tolerant than the pro-government Afrikaans newspapers by a hair or two, were spooked and rejected their earlier support for an ANC stay-at-home. There were depressing divisions within organizations fighting for change, too: the PAC, for example, urged people to reject the stay-at-home conducted by their political rivals. But the Republic Day stayaway, although hundreds of thousands of people participated, didn't go as well as Mandela hoped, perhaps because it was

Singing out. One of Mandela's favourite musicians, Miriam Makeba, testified about apartheid before the United Nations in 1963. The South African Government revoked her citizenship and right of return, making her homeless, until Mandela was finally released.

difficult to organize people while slipping from safe house to safe house. He called off the strike, depressed and disheartened. But he did not give up; he changed tactics. The sun was setting on the time of non-violent struggle.

Mandela had been thinking about a military struggle against white domination for a long time. His first effort to suggest openly that the ANC should follow a military path, made at a low-level meeting, was shot down in flames by some of his closest colleagues, including Moses Kotane, who had sat beside him as a fellow accused in the treason trial. "This will expose innocent people to enemy fire," Kotane said critically. Even Mandela's close friend Sisulu watched and said nothing. Mandela erupted at him later for not supporting him openly.

Sisulu "laughed and said it would have been as foolish as attempting to fight a pride of angry lions," Mandela recounted in his autobiography. But Sisulu, ever the calm strategist, brought the two together for a chat. If you wait for the ideal moment, for textbook conditions, we will be waiting forever,

Mandela argued. We have no choice, he said: "Sebatana ha se bokwe ka diatla" – "The attacks of wild beasts cannot be averted with only bare hands." He won. At the next meeting, Mandela was told to head to Durban to raise formally and quietly the issue of armed struggle with the top leaders of the ANC.

In sub-tropical Durban, Mandela argued that violence was inescapable and that the organization needed to attack symbols of oppression in order to prevent angry people from attacking the oppressors themselves. "Non-violence has not failed us, we have failed non-violence," one critic scolded him. His response was that non-violence had failed the people. But his deeply religious leader, Chief Albert Luthuli, was not convinced. People joined the ANC because of its policy of non-violence, and here was a hothead radical arguing for a complete change in policy without being able to consult with the membership, the elderly Luthuli countered.

But eventually, reluctantly, Luthuli agreed to sidestep this issue. He gave Mandela permission to form an independent military organization. Mandela would retain his membership in the ANC but the ANC would remain wedded to the policy of non-violence and would not be responsible for this new military force. In November 1961, Mandela's new baby was named "Mkhonto we Sizwe", or "The Spear of the Nation", in honour of the warriors of old. It was to become better known by its first two letters: "MK".

Nelson Mandela was one of "the fastest to get to grips with the harsh realities of the African struggle against the most powerful adversary in Africa," said Tambo. Mandela was up against "a highly industrialized, well-armed state, manned by a fanatical group of white men determined to defend their privilege and their prejudice, and aided by the complicity of American, British, West German and Japanese investment in the most profitable system of oppression on the continent".

Mandela quickly set to work, recruiting war veterans and modelling MK on the 1940s Jewish national underground organization operating in Palestine. Since he didn't have an army, he decided to start with low-level sabotage, just a step or two up from vandalism, with strict instructions not to progress further until all avenues of sabotage were exhausted. He paid particular attention to the bitter lessons of the Anglo-Boer wars. More than half a century after the last of the wars between the English and the Afrikaaner, the death toll had ensured an ongoing harvest of resentment and hatred. War was coming, he was convinced of that; but a war with as few losers as possible was his goal. It was an era when it seemed that guerrilla warfare could yield positive results with very little effort – and a minimum of damage. Reality turned out to be a little different.

He promptly put the ANC into an extremely difficult position. In recognition of the ANC's commitment to non-violent change, the 1961 Nobel Peace Prize was awarded to Chief Albert Luthuli. The humble chief joked, when finally let out of the country to accept his award, that the prize united him with the ruling white government: neither he nor they thought he deserved it. Yet the day after Luthuli returned from Norway, Mandela arranged for a

International attention: Sharpeville would turn the world's gaze to South Africa.

Basil D'Oliviera was nominated as one of South Africa's best cricketers of the 20th century, although he never played for his country as he was considered mixed race. South Africa refused to play England in 1968 because D'Oliveira was on the squad. They didn't play international cricket again for a quarter of a century.

series of small explosions to rock unoccupied government offices and electric power stations in the car manufacturing town of Port Elizabeth, in Durban, and gold-crazy Johannesburg. It marked the end of an era.

Mandela had carefully chosen a public holiday known as Blood River, a distasteful day which commemorated the 1838 revenge attack by white Afrikaaners on the Zulu King, Dingane, on the banks of the Ncome River, which ran so red with the blood of the dead that it was renamed by the victors. This event, to many Christian whites, was interpreted as a clear sign of God's support. But many black South Africans saw the Afrikaaners not as the chosen people but more as thieves who stole another's land; they mourned Blood River as a defining moment when military power controlled who owned the land.

It was during this holiday that a handful of homemade bombs went off and thousands of neatly typed, carbon-copied pamphlets appeared, both announcing the birth of MK in the words of Nelson Mandela: "The time comes in the life of any nation when there remain only two choices – submit or fight. That time has now come to South Africa. We shall not submit and we have no choice but to hit back by all means in our power in defence of our people, our future, and our freedom."

Mkhonto we Sizwe warned: "The people's patience is not endless…." But while militant youth were delighted, Mandela was roasted both inside and outside the ANC. Many senior black activists thought Mandela and his handful of conspirators were impatient, juvenile, reckless and out of control. Already, there had been casualties due to the inexpertise of the new military cells: one supporter was dead and another injured after their bomb detonated early.

In many ways, they crossly pointed out, MK was a public relations disaster. The sabotage campaign was meant to alert South Africa's white population to the pressing needs of their fellow black citizens. Although no whites had died, many white people who had been supporters of the claim for gradually extending voting rights were so shocked by the news of the explosions that they now supported the government under any circumstances.

Mandela's argument was that at least now freedom fighters knew who was on their side – and who was against. In October, three months prior to any MK bombs, the same white voters kept the racist fanatics of the National Party in power in a landslide victory. Consistently, since the first post World War II elections in 1948, the white voters had chosen to ignore the kinder, gentler forms of racism advocated by other parties and had gone for the most extreme, totalitarian shape possible. It was the voters who had become aggressive, Mandela said. He was only reacting to their brutality.

There was no turning back. Mandela was not expelled. Instead, the shell-shocked senior leadership of both the Communist Party and the ANC, although officially banned, quietly brought MK – and its headstrong leader – back into the fold. They faced the very real possibility that the ANC would be left behind as an increasingly angry and resentful population moved forward on its own. In 1960, there were riots in Cato Manor, the low-income suburb of Hindi-speaking Indians and Zulu-

speaking Africans wedged into a flood-prone valley in Durban. In rural Pondoland, farmers were openly rebelling against the heavy-handed imposition of another layer of white control, known as the Bantu authorities. This was no longer a people willing to wait indefinitely.

The South African government ridiculed the explosions as the work of amateurs, which was of course true. It also decided to exterminate the ringleaders – especially when more bombs went off two weeks later on New Year's Eve. New legislation was introduced, including the Sabotage Act, which brought in the death sentence for these amateur bomb-makers. The government also defined an illegal gathering in terms so extraordinarily broad that an activist could – and would – be arrested for

having a cup of tea with a friend, or attending the cinema. Mandela's fellow treason trialist, the feisty Helen Joseph, was the first person to be placed under house arrest. Neither of them could imagine that it would last until she turned 80.

Mandela had a new year's resolution to mark the beginning of 1962: it was time to become a soldier. The first batch of would-be soldiers left for military training outside South Africa.

After ten months on the run, he temporarily left the country too, after spending the night with his wife in the Johannesburg home of some discreet white friends. Resigned to her fate, Winnie brought her husband yet another suitcase of clothes and in many ways "behaved as much like a soldier as a wife", he later said.

Police break up one of the riots in Cato Manor, the low-income suburb of Hindi-speaking Indians and Zulu-speaking Africans wedged into a flood-prone valley behind Durban's hilltop university campus.

Mandela followed the driver routine north to the Bechuanaland protectorate, which had been carved out by the escaping Tambo long ago. As a wanted man, so close to the border, he took care to keep his profile low. The absence of any kind of travel documents in either his real or his underground identities proved to be another bureaucratic nightmare.

Tambo, as ANC leader in exile, had been notified that "a family chat" was looming. He was desperately trying to help his old comrade. "Where is Nelson?" he anxiously asked the supportive journalist in Dar es Salaam, the coastal capital of Tanzania, who had organized his own asylum and was helping with the increasing number of South African refugees who made it this far north. Frene Ginwala obligingly dug out the Mandela passport photograph she had slid between her own family's papers and said that "shortly afterwards, a towering figure, heavily built and wearing a conical grass Basotho hat and large mosquito boots loomed on her doorstep". It was Nelson Mandela, who missed out on his much wanted reunion with his old friend owing to a comedy of errors which included outwitting suspected kidnappers, rogue elephants, waterlogged landing strips and rough weather.

While in Tanganyika (now Tanzania), however, the opportunity to lobby for his fledgling army was too good to resist, although he was taken aback when the newly independent country's first president suggested postponing the armed struggle until the more glamorous PAC leader, the pipe-smoking Robert Sobukwe, came out of jail. Mandela politely refused, and poverty-stricken Tanzania went on to become one of the strongest supporters of the struggle for democracy in South Africa.

1962 was the first time Mandela had ever lived without racial segregation. By then the entire system of apartheid was so pervasive, so poisonous, that even this noted revolutionary fell into its trap. Mandela experienced a moment of utter panic when he discovered that the pilot who was going to fly him and other ANC colleagues from Sudan to Ethiopia was black. "I had never seen a black pilot before … how could a black man fly a plane?" he wrote. "I had fallen into the apartheid mind-set, thinking Africans were inferior and that

flying was a white man's job." Over on the west coast, he finally met with Tambo in Ghana, to explain the shift to military struggle. Tambo backed him to the hilt.

In Ethiopia, in front of delegates and leaders from many African states, Mandela went public for the first time. "I have just come out of South Africa, having for the last ten months lived in my own country as an outlaw, away from family and friends," he said to loud cheers in the imperial city, Addis Ababa. He announced that he was not in exile but would return to the country he loved so much. Then he went underground again.

Mandela continued to tour the independent parts of Africa as a kind of high-ranking beggar, surviving on the kindness of friends and diplomats. While he secured cash and promises of more for weapons and training, he also discovered to his surprise that many organizations – including some

The African military: Mozambique president Samora Machel on parade. Mandela would go on to marry Machel's widow.

> "I had fallen into the apartheid mind-set, thinking Africans were inferior and that flying was a white man's job."

from South Africa, such as the rival PAC – described him as a communist puppet who used black bodies as cannon fodder. This was the same accusation that the white government in South Africa was making. After lobbying in a series of Arabic-speaking North African countries, he was struck by the views of an Algerian who noted that their guerrilla warfare waged recently against the French occupiers was not actually designed to win a military victory: it was meant to "unleash political and economic forces that would bring down the enemy". The Algerian said that international public opinion, in this era of mass media, was worth more than a fleet of jet engines. Mandela took this advice to heart.

After the Senegalese president provided him with a diplomatic passport and paid for a plane flight from Dakar to London, Mandela quietly slipped into the United Kingdom to raise support, successfully,

Following page:
Mandela was surprised to find in London that the British press were describing the ANC as a party of the past.

for the struggle for freedom, and discovered that some liberal British newspapers were describing the ANC as a party of the past – not a party with a future. His abundant charm and persuasiveness did much to counter this view, but also alerted the South African government, and their friends, to his presence.

Then he slipped out, just as quietly, to return to Ethiopia for what was meant to be half a year of strenuous military training. The lawyer was about to become a soldier, at the grand old age of 44. He learnt how to use automatic guns, fire mortars and how to make small bombs and mines. He underwent fatigue marches, armed with a gun, bullets and water, when he was ordered to reach a certain point within a limited time. It was a far cry from the legal offices of Mandela and Tambo.

Two months later, a telegram arrived saying the newly formed soldiers of Mkhonto we Sizwe – 21 in all – needed their commander at their makeshift training ground in Tanzania. Carrying a small fortune in cash, with two hundred rounds of ammunition wrapped around his waist and an

automatic pistol concealed inside his jacket holster, he flew southwards to Tanzania. "It was the first time that I was ever saluted by my own soldiers," the commander-in-chief marvelled. In the 18 months following its launch, MK sent more than 100 recruits out of the country for military training. Thousands would follow – even though many disgruntled would-be soldiers were diverted to the classroom, with strict orders that liberation required education.

The Tanzanian Government arranged for a small plane to drop Mandela in Bechuanaland, where a sympathetic white magistrate warned him that the South African police had been informed of his movements. He crossed the border at midnight in his favourite disguise, as a chauffeur for a white theatre director, who had a walk-on part as a member of the multiracial Mkhonto we Sizwe. They reached the ANC safe house, Liliesleaf Farm, in the morning, prepared to carrying on life underground.

He came home to discover that the security police had been constantly harassing his wife in the belief that she would know when her husband had

Protests over Mandela's re-arrest and sentence.

Ruth First, a South African journalist, spent 117 days in solitary detention. Here she speaks in Trafalgar Square.

returned. He also returned to bitter accusations by colleagues that he was dumping the multiracial alliance set up against the government by bowing to the national and ethnic fears of other African nations. He found it difficult to explain how many newly independent states were bewildered by the ANC's commitment to working across racial barriers, and deeply hostile to its historical ties with communists. Beggars can't be choosers, he responded. The ANC has to appear independent of its alliance partners. It has to be first among equals. Otherwise the PAC will continue to capture the world's imagination.

Then the first mistake was made. This is a serious suggestion, said the other members of the military high command. You must go to the leader, Chief Luthuli, who was confined by bans to coastal Natal. Don't go, warned a lone voice, that of Govan Mbeki, who urged Mandela to send a deputy. It was simply too risky. Too dangerous. His warning was

overruled. After all, Mandela had succeeded in life on the run for an astonishing 17 months. What could go wrong?

Luthuli, ill, old and suffering from an excess of attention from the police, managed to meet secretly with Mandela in the house of an Indian woman in the small town of Groutville. The Nobel laureate disliked the idea of being dictated to by foreign powers but said he would consider Mandela's proposition. That Saturday evening, Mandela attended a party given by friends and supporters in Durban, which he described as partly a welcome home from his travels abroad as well as a farewell party because he was returning to Johannesburg.

It was indeed a farewell party. On Sunday, not even halfway home, three carloads of waiting policemen ambushed their car and the over-confident chauffeur – by then sitting in the passenger seat – and his white "boss" – who was driving – were both arrested.

CHAPTER 6

"Esiquithini" – "At the Island"

On a normally quiet news day, newspaper headlines in large black type boasted: "Police swoop ends two years on the run" and "Nelson Mandela under arrest". The number one man on the state's Most Wanted List had been caught.

Mandela had been planning to return to Johannesburg to consult with activists. On Monday, the police did this for him. Locked in a familiar police station, where he had been held as a protestor or visited as a lawyer, he heard a familiar cough. His close friend Walter Sisulu had also been arrested.

"We laughed with an indescribable mixture of relief, surprise, disappointment and happiness," Mandela said. The two spent the night going over the implications of his arrest, the latest in political and military negotiations, and his strategy in court. The friends were soon separated in similar trials but this one night proved hugely important for the struggle. A year later, out on bail while appealing against a six-year sentence, Sisulu took up Mandela's job. He went underground as a full-time leader of the armed struggle.

Mandela was being charged with leaving the country without a valid travel permit, and encouraging workers to go on strike; the authorities were clearly ignorant of his military involvement. On Tuesday morning, Mandela realized that his most powerful weapon was himself: the white magistrate, who knew Mandela professionally, wouldn't make eye contact with him. The white attorneys fidgeted. Mandela had a revelation: "these men were not only uncomfortable because I was a colleague brought low but because I was an ordinary man being punished for his beliefs ... I was the symbol of justice in the court of the oppressor." He announced that he would defend himself.

Crowds surged outside the courtroom. Supporters shouted, "Amandla!" – "Power!" The crowd roared back, "Ngawethu!" – "Is ours!" Police took notes and a few days later, all gatherings held to protest any arrest or trial were outlawed.

Although the authorities did their best to harass Mandela, putting him in cells with notorious gangsters, shuttling him without notice between Johannesburg and Pretoria cells and courtrooms, nobody gave up. His wife arrived twice a week with meals and clean clothes. Supporters brought so much food he shared it with the warders. And he began to study by correspondence course for an advanced legal degree that would allow him to appear in court as an advocate – if he ever got out of court, of course.

By October 1962, a campaign began which was to last for decades. "Free Mandela!" was scrawled on the sides of buildings. The man in question entered the court on the first day of the hearing dressed as a prince with a traditional leopard skin tossed over his shoulder. In the spectators' gallery, his wife held herself high in a beaded headdress and an ankle-length Xhosa skirt.

The prisoner explained that he was not morally bound to obey laws made by a parliament that refused to represent him. "I hate racial discrimination most intensely and in all its manifestations," Mandela lectured the magistrate. "I have fought it all my life. I fight it now and I will do so until the end of my days." His words did not travel far beyond the courtroom. A new piece

The country's most famous lawyer had a new daytime job: sewing and patching old canvas mailbags.

of government legislation imposed heavy fines on any newspaper that ran a quotation from a banned person.

In an astonishing and audacious move, Mandela announced that he was not calling any defence witnesses. How could he? The state's evidence was solid and he had no intention of blaming other colleagues for his own work. That day, the United Nations general assembly voted for the first time to apply sanctions against the South African Government. The same day, Mkhonto we Sizwe soldiers sabotaged government installations in Port Elizabeth and Durban, as if to let their commander know that his work would continue. The next day, he received the stiffest sentence ever handed out in South Africa for a political offence: five years, with no chance of parole.

> Robben Island ... Mandela had seen it from Table Mountain during a visit in 1948. Now he was to see it up close.

Mandela was held for weeks in a constantly lit isolation cell in a grim red-brick Pretoria jail after protesting at being forced to wear shorts and at the inadequate diet of cold porridge. Eventually on the edge of a breakdown and on the verge of initiating conversations with cockroaches, he relented. By the time he had served nine months of his sentence, Mandela would lose more than 25lb after being in and out of solitary confinement.

Held with other, more militant political prisoners from the rival PAC, the country's most famous lawyer had a new daytime job: sewing and patching old canvas mailbags. One night in May a warder ordered him to get his things ready quickly. He was being transferred somewhere very beautiful, a colonel told him lightly. "Die eiland." The island.

There is only one island in South Africa that doesn't need a name – a narrow, flat, wind-whipped outcrop pounded incessantly by the cold Atlantic Ocean surf just 18 miles from the twinkling lights of the country's oldest city, Cape Town. Robben Island has been a leper colony, a lunatic asylum and a naval base during World War II, and already held nearly 1000 prisoners. Mandela had seen it from Table Mountain during a visit in 1948. Now he was to see it up close.

But first, further humiliation and embarrassment awaited this proud and fastidious man. Four prisoners were shackled together and held in a windowless van that contained only a sanitary bucket. They were driven all night and arrived at the wooden docks of Cape Town in the late afternoon, frustrated, hungry, smelly and soiled. Shoved into the ferry, still shackled, the quartet of prisoners was placed in the rickety hold with a porthole above them. Laughing warders urinated on them through the gap.

As the ferry docked, they were greeted by angry warders shouting: "Dis die Eiland! Hier gaan julle vrek!" – "This is the Island! Here you will die!" If Mandela spoke in English, sneering warders would reply in Afrikaans, "I don't understand that kaffir-lover's language." In Pretoria, Mandela had insisted on negotiating for better prison conditions, to the disgust of other political prisoners. "Ah," spat one, "Mandela is a little boy who is afraid of the white man." Here, he succeeded in a small act of defiance almost as soon as his feet touched the island soil. While warders shouted at him in the same terms used to hurry up ambling cattle, he quietly and quickly persuaded the other three prisoners to embark on a go-slow. He ambled into his new home while warders grew purple in the face from shouting.

Punishment came immediately. Mandela was forced to strip naked in front of the warders and the other new prisoners in a room deliberately filled with several inches of water. As each item of clothing came off, the warders searched it and threw it into the water. Then he was told to fetch the clothes out of the water and put them on. It was going to be a long five years, he thought.

"Our house is on fire," warned Sisulu in June 1963 in an illicit radio broadcast after he had gone

Robben Island Prison in 2002.

NELSON MANDELA

An historical photo of two lines of inmates in the bleak prison yard, Robben Island.

underground. "There is no time to stand and watch. Thousands are in jail, including our dynamic Nelson Mandela … Robben Island is a giant concentration camp for political prisoners."

And yet soon after being smuggled to Robben Island, Mandela was suddenly brought back to the Pretoria cells without explanation. He began to glimpse colleagues who had been smuggled out of the country earlier. His attempts to contact lawyers were met with the news that the lawyers themselves had been detained without trial. Then he saw friends such as Sisulu from the Rivonia farm underground headquarters and he knew what had happened.

"We have broken the back of the ANC," boasted the South African Minister of Justice. Almost the entire leadership of the armed wing of the ANC had been caught by police hiding in a dry cleaner's van. Apparently, a detainee who was cracking up under the strain of the new 90-day detention without trial legislation had sold out his colleagues for 3000 rands.

Others on the run were soon mopped up. The activists had not realized that the South African Government had been talking to their counterparts in the French and Portuguese secret police in other African colonies. The new interrogation techniques were ruthless. Accused number nine, Elias

Motsoaledi, a low-level member of the military wing, was tortured. The last of the accused, Andrew Mlangeni, who came from a Soweto family so poor that he began work at the age of 12, was assaulted and tortured with electric shocks even though he, too, was only a junior member.

The prisoners faced sabotage rather than treason charges. Under the sabotage legislation, and unlike the earlier treason trial, the onus was now on the defence to prove the accused were innocent. Each of the Rivonia trialists was accused of 222 acts of sabotage between 1961 and 1963 in preparation for guerrilla warfare. The state asked for the maximum penalty: death by hanging.

To avoid the death sentence, they would have to convince the judge that they had not decided on guerrilla warfare, and that they had tried to avoid taking human life during the sabotage campaign.

On December 3, 1963, Mandela, now allowed to wear a suit, was asked to plead. "My Lord, it is not I but the government which should be in the dock," accused number one responded gravely. "I plead not guilty." The other seven accused reacted in the same manner. The state was on trial. Foreign television crews were filming outside. High-ranking diplomats observed from the gallery. Night-long prayer vigils were being held in London's famous St Paul's Cathedral. The world was watching.

Police stand guard on the steps of the Pretoria Supreme Court in 1964.

Following page:
Mandela had put the South African Government on trial. Together with the crowd assembled outside Pretoria's Supreme Court, the world held its breath for the outcome.

NELSON MANDELA

Mandela was calm. He had been out of the country for much of the time span. The government had even managed to accuse him of sabotage efforts conducted after his arrest. So it was a bitter blow to discover that some of his colleagues, more concerned with history than with safety, had retained incriminating notes and documents in his own handwriting, even though they had been told to destroy them.

He was also saddened to see that one of his Durban colleagues in the armed struggle, Bruno Mtolo, a handyman and electrician whose skills had come in handy when it was time to blow up power pylons and electricity lines, had happily turned state witness. As Mtolo was one of the last people to see Mandela in Durban, it solved the mystery of how the police knew where he had been. Informers, whether operating from ego, ideology or under threat of torture, were to bedevil the freedom struggle for decades.

The state ended its case in February 1964. This was the last chance for the accused to clear their names. But Mandela shocked the prosecutor by refusing to engage in the expected stop-start cat-and-mouse routine of question and answer. That task was for his colleagues. Rather than give evidence in the witness stand, Mandela opted to make a statement from the dock. It may have been the riskiest thing he ever did.

April 20, 1964 was a wet and miserable Monday. Mandela's elderly mother and his young wife sat side by side in the Palace of Justice. His mother had come up all the way from the rural Transkei to watch her only son stand up and begin calmly with the words, "I am the first accused."

Mandela made it clear at the very beginning that he was nobody's puppet: "The suggestion made by the State in its opening that the struggle in South Africa is under the influence of foreigners or communists is wholly incorrect. I have done whatever I did, both as an individual and as a leader of my people, because of my experience in South Africa and my own proudly felt African background, and not because of what any outsider might have said."

Reading from his own script, carefully drafted over two weeks after the trial ended, Mandela

admitted immediately that he helped to form and run a military operation but argued that he was judiciously using sabotage in order to prevent a greater evil from occurring: "Violence by the African people had become inevitable, and that unless responsible leadership was given to canalize and control the feelings of our people, there would be outbreaks of terrorism which would produce an intensity of bitterness and hostility between the various races of this country which is not produced even by war."

But he denied that he was a terrorist. He had not embarked on preparations for full-scale guerrilla warfare. "We believe that South Africa belongs to all the people who live in it, and not to one group, be it black or white. We did not want an interracial war, and tried to avoid it to the last minute."

In some detail, he lectured the courtroom as if he were an expert witness and a historian of note rather than a convicted criminal with every expectation that he would soon be swinging lifeless from a noose: "We had either to accept a permanent state of inferiority, or to defy the government. We chose to defy the law."

He told the state that he would not reveal who he worked with, or what they did, when they embarked on "properly-controlled violence", and gave a detailed history of the sabotage campaign. After an hour, Sisulu quietly handed a glass of water to Mandela. He went on, inexorable.

Reading slowly in English, he told the spellbound courtroom, "The initial plan was based on a careful analysis of the political and economic situation of our country. We believed that South Africa depended to a large extent on foreign capital and foreign trade. We felt that planned destruction of power plants, and interference with rail and telephone communications, would tend to scare away capital from the country, make it more difficult for goods from the industrial areas to reach the seaports on schedule, and would in the long run be a heavy drain on the economic life of the country, thus compelling the voters of the country to reconsider their position."

Outside, a fine drizzle descended on Pretoria. It was dark in the courtroom. Everyone was mesmerized, even the prosecutor. Women in the section reserved for non-Europeans were openly weeping as Mandela came to his parting words, which had so frightened his lawyers that one warned, "If Mandela reads this in court they will take him straight out to the back of the courthouse and string him up."

Mandela refused to change his parting words. He put his script down on the table and turned to face

In post-apartheid South Africa, millions still battle with poverty, one of the legacies of oppressive rule. Brenda Mashila is pictured on the five-kilometre walk to school and playing in rubbish outside her home in rural Johannesburg. In 1992, the family did not have running water or electricity.

NELSON MANDELA

"… an ideal for which I am prepared to die."

the judge. He did not break eye contact as he spoke the final risky words engraved in his memory: "I have fought against white domination, and I have fought against black domination. I have cherished the ideal of a democratic and free society in which all persons live together in harmony and with equal opportunities. It is an ideal, which I hope to live for and to achieve. But if needs be, it is an ideal for which I am prepared to die."

It was the last time the judge looked his famous prisoner in the eye. Mandela finished. The courtroom was silent. Even the aggressive, jumpy prosecutor was quiet. Mandela had been speaking for hours. He sat down. One of the world's great speeches was over.

"When he said, 'I am prepared to die,' I did not realise that tears were pouring down my face," said Walter Sisulu's indomitable wife Albertina, a hardened nurse not given to emotional outbursts.

Despite the restrictions on quoting banned people, a daily Johannesburg newspaper printed his speech almost word for word. Ever since, there has always been someone, somewhere in the country, who could quote the final paragraph.

For three weeks, the judge pondered his verdict. In the outside world, the United Nations Security Council urged the government to give Mandela and his colleagues amnesty – although both the United States and the United Kingdom chose to abstain from voting. In South Africa, Mandela wrote some of the papers for his University of London examinations to become an advocate – and passed, baffling his guards. "Would he use it where he was going?" they wondered aloud. Meanwhile, all the Rivonia trialists told their stunned lawyers that there would be no appeal, even if they were given the death sentence, even for the junior members. "Our message was that no sacrifice was too great in the struggle for freedom," Mandela said.

On Friday June 12, 1964, Mandela entered the familiar courtroom for the last time, nearly a year since the Rivonia raid. The nervous judge mumbled, "I have decided not to impose the supreme penalty … The sentence in the case of all of the accused will be one of life imprisonment." Mandela turned to the spectators, smiling broadly, but in the chaos he could see neither his wife nor his mother. Police pushed him down the stairs to the underground holding cells, where he was handcuffed. When the crowd outside did not leave, the Rivonia convicts were thrown into their black van. They pushed their clenched fists out through the window bars, hoping they could be seen. Then the iron doors of Pretoria Central clanged shut behind them.

On the same day, Mandela's old legal partner issued a statement in Tanzania. "The judge in the trial has done his duty to the white government which appointed him," said Oliver Tambo. "The Rivonia leaders have done their duty to South Africa and all its people. They have done their duty to Africa and the world. Those who opposed evil have been put away by the evildoers."

He made a terrible but accurate prediction. "Since in South Africa moderation and reason leads only to … death cells and torture chambers, moderation and reason must take leave of the South African situation," Tambo said. "Their imprisonment is not the end of the liberation struggle or of resistance to tyranny; it is the beginning of a new and decisive phase." But he warned that the next stage may "embroil the continent of Africa and destroy the foundations of international peace".

The authorities liked to operate at night. One midnight, Mandela was awake in his solitary cell when the colonel in charge whispered that he was a lucky man. "We are taking you to a place where you will have your freedom," he was told. He knew he was returning to the Island, for a much longer time. This time the Rivonia trial convicts were flown directly to the island in a military transport plane.

But now he was held in a prison within a prison: a special one-story rectangle where single cells flanked both edges of a corridor on all but one side. On the fourth wall, guards with guns and dogs

patrolled a high catwalk. A cement courtyard marked the centre.

The 2ft-thick walls leaked moisture. The blankets were so threadbare they were see-through. The mattress was a thin straw mat. The light bulb burned day and night. The only toilet was a 10-inch wide iron bucket with a dip in the porcelain lid that was meant to store water for washing hands. Mandela could only walk three steps before he reached the opposite wall of his cell. It was so small that when he lay down, both his feet and his head touched concrete.

Mandela was the 466th prisoner admitted to the island in 1964. He was 46 years old, and his new job was to take stones the size of volleyballs and crush them into gravel with a hammer, all in total silence. In the next year, he would be forced to mine limestone from the island quarry. The quarry job would last 13 years, interspersed with occasional truck trips to the island shoreline to harvest slimy, heavy knots of seaweed for fertilizer. It would permanently damage his eyesight.

Prisoners were not allowed to talk. Watches and clocks were banned. There were no longer black warders. There were no white prisoners. And political prisoners were not allowed to mix with ordinary prisoners. The loneliness was devastating. As the lowest class of prisoner, Mandela was allowed one visitor every six months. He was also allowed to write a letter every six months, and receive one letter every six months, as long as these were from close family relatives. Many letters went astray – or were so censored that they looked more like artwork than words.

After Mandela had spent three months on the island, at the end of August, Winnie finally received permission as a banned activist to leave Johannesburg and meet her husband. They spoke for half an hour but could not touch. She would not be allowed to visit again for two years.

The struggle carried on, in miniature rather than the international framework he had envisaged. "I was in a different and smaller arena, an arena for whom the only audience was ourselves and our oppressors," is how Mandela remembered the dark years. "We would fight inside as we would fight outside."

Winnie with Mandela's mother, Fanny, outside the Pretoria Supreme Court, after the life imprisonment verdict is handed down.

CHAPTER 7

The Path to Freedom

Communication was a nightmare. Even speaking to general prisoners held in the non-political sections of the island relied on huge amounts of effort and luck. The political prisoners would write tiny coded messages on discarded matchboxes. The messages would be left at the crossroads where the prisoners separated to different quarries. Rain was the ruin of many an urgent message.

Brief whispered conversations could only happen when the metal drums of cold, watery food were delivered by the prisoners. Soon plastic-wrapped notes were surfacing in the dregs of food and in the deliberately dirty dishes being returned to the prisoners on kitchen duty. Other notes were wrapped in plastic and taped to the inside rim of toilets. Milk was a rare treat – because notes written in milk looked blank after drying, the letters to reappear when sprayed with the disinfectant used by the prisoners to de-louse their cells. Thin scraps of toilet paper were used so much that the prisoners were rationed to eight squares a day.

Communication with the outside world was equally strenuous. Gossip from the hospital wing, where the prisoners mingled, helped keep Mandela up to date. Prisoners who were due for release had to memorize dozens of messages or smuggle out notes. Lawyers were supposed to be given confidential access to their clients, so no warders were present, but the room was bugged, so Mandela would have a conversation with long pauses, when he would write down the nickname of the message's intended recipient. Some messages would find their way to the distant Oliver Tambo,

and in this way the inside and outside wings of the liberation movement remained in tentative, agonizing contact. Homesick Tambo would respond, with messages about "clubs" and "the family". The prisoners were clear that they could not control the fight for freedom from Robben Island. And Tambo was equally clear that he would not accept the position of President of the ANC while most of its leadership was locked away.

Later, fresh prisoners themselves brought news. The six members of the "mini Rivonia trial" were

> Milk was a rare treat – because notes written in milk looked blank after drying ...

locked up after being charged with 177 counts of sabotage, and served around a dozen years each. Mkhonto we Sizwe soldiers arrived from their first combat effort, a disastrous expedition in 1967 to try to find a safe route over thousands of kilometres that separated independent Tanzania from South Africa. There was even an international prison contingent: in 1971, soldiers fighting for the independence of neighbouring Namibia (then called South West Africa and controlled by South Africa) were also put into the isolation wards.

However, Mandela was well informed about the intense harassment of his wife. Neatly cut-out clippings from newspapers would be placed on his

NELSON MANDELA

bedding by warders. One security officer had broken into her bedroom while she was dressing, and when she angrily pushed him out, she was charged with assault. Soon, she would be tortured. Relations with his eldest three children were fraught. His eldest son, Thembi, was only 16 when his father was sent to jail, but hurt by his mother's divorce, alienated from Mandela's second wife and torn between politics and faith, he chose to stay away. The other children were too young to be allowed visiting rights: it might be psychologically harmful, the government said.

Newspapers were like gold. Mac Maharaj, then considered the most tortured political detainee in the country, blackmailed a corrupt warder to bring him a daily newspaper for six months. Another inmate, Eddie Daniels, serving a 15-year sentence, took to stealing newspapers from visiting preachers. Not until 1978 would the prison authorities allow censored news reports to be read across the in-house radio system. Not until 1980 were the prisoners granted the right to buy newspapers – and even these were censored by scissor-wielding warders.

In 1968 Mandela turned 50. Many activists – even some policemen and warders – had expected that by now the Rivonia prisoners would be freed and living in a democracy. But it was not to be. "Whenever I'm asked when the revolution will come to South Africa, I always say, 'in 3 years time'," joked Joe Slovo, a founding member of the military wing who spent 27 years in exile.

Family worries preyed on his mind. Mandela was visited by his frail mother, and his teenage son and daughter from his first marriage. Several weeks later, he received a telegram from his youngest son, informing him that his mother Fanny was dead of a heart attack. The prison authorities would not let him attend the funeral, saying they feared the possibility of a rescue team abducting him.

The following year another telegram revealed that Mandela's first son and heir to the Madiba clan, had been killed in a car accident in the Transkei. Thembi was just 25, a husband and the father of two small children.

At the same time, Winnie had been dragged away from her two small daughters and was being

A rare moment on Robben Island: Mandela and Sisulu confer.

Following page:
1994: Mandela revisits the view from the cell where he was incarcerated for 18 of his 27 years in jail.

brutally interrogated in solitary confinement in Pretoria by the authorities, who were convinced that she had set up some sort of communication system with her husband.

Mandela lay on his bed mat for hours. Walter Sisulu came by and held his hand, saying nothing. The happy baby Mandela had so loved bathing, feeding and telling stories to, the confident child who would tease his father for not working hard enough in the boxing ring, the good student who became withdrawn after his parents' divorce, the brave boy who had worn his father's old jacket and vowed to "take care of the family" while his father was underground: he was dead – and his father could do absolutely nothing.

"I was already overwrought about my wife, I was still grieving for my mother, and then to hear such news…" Mandela said later. "It left a hole in my heart that can never be filled." Again, permission to attend the funeral was denied.

The world moved on without him. In 1972, security policemen kicked down the door of his old house in Soweto, throwing bricks through the windows and firing guns before charging Winnie with the crime of working at a lawyer's office in defiance of banning orders, which allowed her to speak only to her daughters or a doctor. She was eventually sentenced to six months in prison. Now the children again had both parents in jail. After Winnie's release in 1975, she faked her eldest daughter's birth documents so that she would seem 16 and receive permission to visit her father. Fifteen-year-old Zindzi hadn't seen Mandela since she was three.

Just as depressing was a family feud, which matched the country's deteriorating politics. A nephew of Mandela's, although slightly older, Kaizer Daliwonga Matanzima had been his mentor long ago at Fort Hare University. Now Matanzima, a traditional leader, had chosen to collaborate with the South African government's obsessive fantasy of inventing rural tribal states, independent countries which remained unrecognized by the outside world and utterly helpless without apartheid funding. Black residents of the cities found themselves stripped of their South African citizenship and forced to move into several ethnically and linguistically divided scraps of land, where many starved. The Transkei,

Winnie, with Joyce Sikhakhane, Zindzi and Iris Xaba, in 1970. Winnie would be arrested, put in solitary confinement and tortured. Zindzi would not see her father for 13 years.

Mandela's home region, was to become the first of these Bantustans or homelands, and Matanzima was to rule there by fear and by force. He even persuaded Winnie's father to become its first minister of agriculture, deepening the family rift. Later, in a bitter irony, Matanzima even deposed the Thembu King Sabata, the very man the young Mandela had been groomed to counsel.

Matanzima often asked to visit Mandela, who refused for decades: "Something snapped inside me when he went over to the Nats," Mandela wrote to a friend. "Indeed, politics have split families, hero and worshipper." There were other unwelcome visitors. In 1976, he received a visit from Jimmy Kruger, the notoriously cold-hearted Minister of Prisons, who made a tempting offer: if Mandela would recognize the Transkei as an independent

state and move there, government would reduce his life sentence. Mandela refused, easily. The offer would be repeated. Later, Kruger would urge Mandela to be reasonable: "We can work with you but not with your colleagues." But Mandela was used to divide and rule tactics by now.

Perhaps it was fortunate that Mandela was protected by prison walls from such ruthless people. Others were less fortunate. The rising Black Consciousness intellectual and author Steve Biko, who might have taken Mandela's place as leader, was savagely beaten to death by government officials in 1977, when he was on the verge of speaking to the ANC in exile. Kruger commented, "I am not glad and I am not sorry about Mr Biko. His death leaves me cold." The National Party delegates applauded him.

Mourners transport the coffin of Black Consciousness Movement leader, Steve Biko. Biko was beaten to death in prison, which made him one of the most influential martyrs in the anti-apartheid movement.

NELSON MANDELA

Youths riot in Johannesburg, 1976. In Soweto, more than 1000 children and teenagers are killed as they protest against being taught in Afrikaans at school. Many cross the border to join Mkhonto we Sizwe, and many more end up on Robben Island.

In 1976, the prisoners heard fresh rumours of violence in Soweto. The government had closed the mission schools and created a dumbed-down education system; now it insisted all lessons for black students would be taught in the Afrikaans language. The angry students marched, the police shot into the crowd, and the crowd fought back. It was another defining moment, and soon Robben Island was filled with angry and almost illiterate young men who knew little and cared less about the ANC greats ensconced there. Soon there were so many prisoners that manual labour ended: It was easier to keep the new rebellious intake in their cells. But despite differences in outlook, the class

of '76 kept Mandela up to date with his own country. The new prisoners also showed the ANC in exile that they were wrong about the armed struggle. The plan had always been to target the rural areas. Now they realized that they could take the fight to the cities.

A year later, Mandela learnt that his wife and last child had been forced into internal exile in a remote seSotho-speaking township outside a small, suspicious town called Brandfort in the conservative Orange Free State. Police loaded her furniture and clothing into the back of a truck and moved Winnie and Zindzi to a shack with no heat, no running water and no toilet. Winnie, already

NELSON MANDELA

damaged by constant police harassment, arrests without trial and brutal beatings, did her best to conceal from her husband how the isolation further warped her spirits. Better news came in 1978, when their elder daughter, although still a teenager, fell in love with and married a Swazi prince. This gave Zenani precious diplomatic status and soon she was allowed to visit – and Mandela was allowed to hold his first grandchild. He did not let go of the baby for the entire visit and named the small girl "Zaziwe"– "Hope".

Whispers continued to spread news. The lifers knew that both nearby Portuguese colonies Angola and Mozambique had received independence. Mandela recognized the pressure this would put on the South African Government. But halfway

The then British Prime Minister, Margaret Thatcher, described Mandela as "a dangerous communist terrorist".

through the1970s, the prisoners heard that South African troops had illegally and secretly invaded Angola on the side of a virulently anti-communist rebel movement. Newly independent, cash-strapped Mozambique found itself fighting a rebel movement funded and equipped by South Africa that would litter the countryside with millions of deadly mines; eventually Mozambique would be begging for peace with South Africa in the Nkomati Accord. In 1981, South African hit squads killed 16 people, including women and children, in Mozambique and a year later used a parcel bomb to assassinate Mandela's long-term friend, Ruth First. In 1982, more assassins slipped over the border of the independent kingdom of Lesotho, killing 42. It seemed like the South African government had

It seemed like the South African government had declared war on the continent ...

declared war on the continent – and anyone who sheltered freedom fighters. Mkhonto we Sizwe responded by setting off its first car bomb at the military and air force headquarters in Pretoria in May 1983. Nineteen people died. Hundreds were injured. South Africa seemed committed to an endless spiral of violence – and nobody was more concerned about this than Mandela. But what could he do about it in jail?

In March 1980, the Johannesburg *Sunday Post* had a two-word headline: "FREE MANDELA". Inside was a petition calling for his release: a clever way around the ban on using his words. This was a breakthrough by Oliver Tambo, who had also accepted a prestigious award from India, on behalf of his silenced friend. Some people within the liberation movement were disturbed by the focus on just one person, when Mandela was in jail with hundreds of other supporters, and Tambo found himself having to explain that he wasn't ignoring the others in favour of his old friend: the "Free Mandela" campaign was using a symbol, the best known of all the many victims of apartheid. Sports and consumer boycotts continued, and economic sanctions were implemented in a patchy way across the world. But nothing happened that would indeed free Mandela – although he was cheered by the fact that anti-apartheid protestors briefed by the ANC abroad were able to force multinational banks to stop lending money to the almost-bankrupt apartheid government. Another financial blow came when American pension funds withdrew their investments in South Africa. But many powerful governments around the world were comfortable operating with the apartheid state: British Prime Minister Margaret Thatcher described Mandela as a dangerous communist terrorist and said that anyone who thought the ANC could form a government was "living in cloud-cuckoo land". Much of the work of freeing Mandela was done inside South Africa.

On a personal level, Mandela sometimes fumbled his relationships with his children, all now adults and parents themselves, putting enormous pressure on them to succeed academically and professionally, refusing to allow visits if they did not meet his orders to follow higher education. It did not go down well. Makgatho, his only surviving son, would give up visiting his father in 1983 and returned to the Transkei to help his mother, Evelyn, run a trading store. His first daughter, Makaziwe, went abroad to study, as did Zenani, his first daughter with Winnie. Some of his most hectoring letters were reserved for Zindzi, a promising poet and a university drop-out who had two children out of wedlock with two different men – one of them violent. He once chastised her for not going to university: "Of all the unspeakable errors you have made in your life, what you have done during the last nine months is the most disastrous." Later, his daughter Makaziwe would have to warn him against interfering in her relationship with her own children. Mandela recognized that his children had lost out on a father long before he went to prison, and that letters were no substitute for his presence. He comforted himself with the thoughts that his marriage had survived – but the truth was that he

> This was a man who never spoke of his own freedom; it was always "We" and "Us" in his letters and conversations.

knew little of how Winnie was being transformed in her own private hell.

In March 1982, after being on the island for 18 years, Mandela was suddenly told to pack up his belongings. Three friends, including Sisulu, were given the same orders. Were they to be freed? Another clumsy attempt at divide-and-rule? The four were hustled into a windowless truck at the Cape Town docks and were driven through a sequence of police checkpoints. The back doors swung open. Mandela was marched down concrete steps and through metal doors. He was at Pollsmoor Prison, and slept on a real bed that night. Two years later, he was allowed to kiss his wife for the first time in more than two decades. But he remained vigilant; he was not convinced that the government wanted to change. In addition, his new home isolated him from many of his old friends. This was a man who never spoke of his own freedom; it was always "we" and "us" in his letters and conversations.

Others, international and local, picked up on Tambo's bid to use Mandela as a symbol of all the prisoners in South Africa. A new organization inside South Africa, the United Democratic Front, an unlikely, unwieldy, fantastically successful coalition, revived the idea of liberation through posters and meetings, humour and song, in 1983. Mandela was named patron. Abroad, people took up the chorus: "Free Nelson Mandela!" But inside South Africa, the townships were on fire and polls showed that many people saw no option but civil war.

Following page:
Marchers hold their banners high for Walter Sisulu after he is freed from Robben Island.

THEIR DUE BE
THEIR SWEAT I
PROPHET
CALL OF ISLA
LONG LIVE ANC!
LIVE ANC!
LONG LIVE ANC
Issued by NRC

In response, in January 1985, the President of South Africa told parliament that he would offer Mandela freedom if he unconditionally renounced violence. In February, Mandela's words were heard in public for the first time in 20 years. His daughter Zindzi read out his reply to a crowded stadium in Soweto, in which he urged the South African President to renounce violence himself.

"Only free men can negotiate," she read to cheers. "Prisoners cannot enter into contracts … I cannot and will not give any undertaking at a time when I and you, the people, are not free. Your freedom and mine cannot be separated. I will return."

The pressure was on. The fight against racism in South Africa had now been going on for three-quarters of a century. And Mandela couldn't pick up the phone to discuss matters with Tambo. Later that year, the Minister of Justice took advantage of Mandela's hospital visit for prostate surgery to drop by and say hello. On his return he was kept separate from his colleagues in another part of Pollsmoor. Now he couldn't strategize with Sisulu, the man who had been his sounding board all his adult life. But Mandela realized that the latest isolation offered the liberation movement a way out: if he overstepped the mark, freedom fighters could just say, "The old man's gone mad." His solitude was so complete that later, when he was taken on escorted trips around Cape Town in order to make his longing for freedom unbearable, nobody recognized him. The last photo of him had been taken decades earlier, in 1962.

The cycle of tentative offers of freedom, undermined by ruthless suppression, continued through 1986. An intensive round of diplomatic efforts was undertaken by representatives of the Commonwealth, who visited Mandela in Cape Town, Tambo in Lusaka and the South African Government in Pretoria. It looked hopeful. But the day before the Commonwealth negotiators were due to meet again with Mandela, the South African President ordered his forces to launch illegal air raid and commando attacks on ANC bases in the neighbouring countries of Botswana and Zimbabwe and as far north as Zambia. When criticized, the President used the American

Government's recent cross-border raids into Libya as an excuse: if they could do it, so could he. Once again, an opportunity to move forward was squandered. Severe martial law dominated 1986, 1987 and 1988 as the townships were surrounded by kilometres of barbed wire, with armed soldiers pointing their guns towards the homes. Thousands were arrested and thrown into jail; anyone left went into hiding. The ANC turned 75 and the white voters returned the National Party to power in another election.

"The most discouraging moments," Mandela once noted, "are precisely the time to launch an initiative." He insisted on being able to speak with his colleagues at Pollsmoor Prison about the possibility of talks. From three different prisoners, he received three different responses. Ever the strategist, Sisulu wanted to know why he was doing all the reaching out and why the government wasn't doing more. Raymond Mhlaba, one of the first to go into exile to receive military training, said: "Should have done this years ago." And the reaction of Ahmed Kathrada, who began his long involvement in the struggle at the age of 12, can best be summed up in one word: "No!" Rumours did the rounds. Soon, even far-off Tambo smuggled a surprisingly hostile note to his old friend through lawyers. "What are you discussing with the government?" it asked. "About the possibility of a meeting between the two enemies," replied Mandela.

"Only free men can negotiate ..."

Secret negotiations were almost as slow as the notes that used to be smuggled around Robben Island. The first formal meeting – government officials in suits, Mandela a thin, almost emaciated figure in prison overalls and boots – was in May 1988. By the end of the year, while recovering from tuberculosis, Mandela was whisked away again from the handful of colleagues who shared prison quarters with him on the mainland, this time to an isolated cottage in the grounds of the Victor Verster prison far away from Cape Town. The house was infested with electronic bugs, even in the flowerbeds. He learnt how to use

Mandela's final days in captivity would be spent in Victor Verster Prison. His house would be infested with electronic bugs.

Sisulu greets local well-wishers on his way home to Soweto after being released from prison.

newfangled technology such as a microwave, began to receive many visitors, was in occasional contact with Tambo abroad as well as his prison colleagues on the Island and at Pollsmoor, and was told that this was his last house before freedom. But, what kind of freedom? Hundreds of detainees were risking death in hunger strikes in protest at being detained without trial for weeks, months and years. What kind of South Africa would be left?

Life works in mysterious ways. In January 1989, the grumpy, suspicious, paranoid President of South Africa, P. W. Botha, had a stroke. Known as the Great Crocodile in Afrikaans, the domineering old man clung to power, reluctantly relinquishing his position as head of party but insisting that he remain president of the country. Halfway through the year, Botha suddenly announced his resignation on national television, accusing his colleagues of stabbing him in the back. A day later, his replacement, a conservative who had resisted many of the in-house attempts to reform apartheid or give it a facelift, was sworn in. On the same day, Mandela wrote to him. "Let us meet," said the message.

Secret negotiations resumed. Clearly some kind of change was in the air. Some of the secret military structures that had been behind hit squads and assassinations were quietly dissolved. The minutely detailed side of apartheid, around since 1953 – the rules governing which beaches people could swim on, which taps they could drink from, which library books they could take out – was on the way out. But nobody was saying anything about one person, one vote – not yet. And international diplomatic pressure was ambivalent, to say the least: one British newspaper noted that "the only thing worse than a free Mandela is a dead Mandela".

Government continued to test the waters. Govan Mbeki, the man whose warning that Mandela should remain in hiding had proved so accurate all those decades ago, was released without restrictions at end of May 1987. One down. Three weeks later, Mbeki was placed under a form of house arrest and confined to Port Elizabeth for stating, in all honesty, that he was an ANC leader. The government clearly wanted puppets, not power-sharing.

Walter Sisulu and three other Rivonia trialists living in Pollsmoor Prison were released to enormous jubilation in October 1989. Others followed. Mandela remained in jail. No black person had the vote and the ANC was still an illegal organization. If he walked out of jail, he would soon be back inside it.

Then, in parliament, in February 1990, the ANC – and 31 other organizations – were unbanned. It was a strange, hopeful, frightening, confusing time. *Impis* – bands of murderous warriors loyal to homeland leaders – still had free rein in many parts of the country, where police and army refused to intervene. Some political prisoners were freed but others were not. The death penalty was suspended. The state of emergency was partly lifted. Troops were still in the townships, the townships were still on fire, and South Africa teetered on the edge of bankruptcy.

In a few days, without warning, Mandela was offered his freedom. He refused. He asked for a few more days in prison to prepare family and colleagues, fearing chaos in the unpredictable turbulence of the times. And after all, what were a few days after so many decades? The government refused. They'd already leaked the information to the foreign media, they whined.

On February 11 he walked free.

CHAPTER 8

"I Feel Like an Old Battery That Has Been Recharged!"

While Mandela was now out of prison, he was far from being a free man. He was a ghost, an enigma, a figure from out of the distant past, an unknown quantity to many – maybe even to his own wife, who had spoken for so long and so eloquently on his behalf. Even as they walked out of prison holding hands, they looked away from each other, at the crowds and the microphones and the television cameras. They would never spend a night together, he would later reluctantly confess.

It was probably the most dangerous moment in the history of the country as decades of pent-up feelings, fears and frustrations were finally aired. In Durban, this author witnessed police shooting buckshot directly at people celebrating the release of "the old man." In Cape Town, resentful youths looted stores and picked people's pockets after Mandela was delayed in making his first public appearance. In Soweto candles were held high in the streets. There were hundreds of children and teenagers, not yet born when he went to jail, singing, "We love you, Nelson Mandela, oh, we love you, Nelson Mandela." They broke the law with every note. Nobody knew what the dawn would bring. Many white South Africans, accustomed to domineering, authoritarian governments, quickly blamed Mandela for not bringing instant peace with him when he walked out of the prison gates. But Mandela had become an obsessive gardener in his long years in prison. He knew that gardens need to be nurtured. The time was not yet ripe.

Mandela's work began immediately, without a single day off to acclimatize. In his own camp, many people were bitter after years of repression

and wanted to intensify the armed struggle now that he was free. Mandela – the original firebrand, the one person who had argued so fiercely for armed struggle all those years ago – soon reduced the role of his own guerrilla army in the struggle for freedom. Although the movement – weakened by spies and betrayal, drained by infighting and years of poverty – barely had the power by now to wield meaningful armed struggle, idealistic South Africans were

A salute of victory as Mandela is finally released.

outraged by his compromise. The state had not given up its soldiers and guns – they were still murdering ordinary people – but here was Mandela, talking peace in exchange for the release of political prisoners who shouldn't have been in jail in the first place. "Madiba," complained one of 25 rebellious Robben Island prisoners who were refusing amnesty, "I have been fighting the government all my life and now I have to ask for a pardon from them?"

It was one of the most complicated balancing acts in modern history. If he didn't bring all his

"I FEEL LIKE AN OLD BATTERY THAT HAS BEEN RECHARGED!"

people with him, Mandela knew that he would meet the fate of many other go-it-alone leaders. He didn't want to become another Mikhail Gorbachev, the Russian leader celebrated for ending communism and then overthrown by the ordinary people whose domestic lives he had turned upside down. Inadvertently, Gorbachev had done Mandela one huge favour: with the thawing of the Cold War and the eventual brick-by-brick dismantling of the Berlin Wall in Germany it was far harder for his opponents to typecast him as a dangerous communist menace. Ironically, while Mandela travelled through Europe, North America and Asia in the months after his release, the one place he didn't visit was the place he had always been accused by his detractors of admiring: the Soviet Union, which was so desperate for money by then that it was getting into bed with the deeply discredited white minority government of South Africa, cutting diamond-dealing contracts under the table and booting out ANC guerrillas. In this new strange new world, so different from the one Mandela had last inhabited, enemies could be friends and friends could be enemies. While he was showered with well-meaning advice from foreign governments, his own view was clear: South Africans got themselves into this mess, South Africans would have to find their own way out.

Many people were afraid that he would leave prison as a tired old man, preserved in the 1950s, but the former convict had a relish for life that wore out his enemies − and his friends. "I feel like an old battery that has been recharged!" he exulted. An exhausted and ill Oliver Tambo had carefully nurtured the ANC for decades in exile, at enormous cost to his own health. Could Mandela keep it together at this vulnerable moment? The movement had been scattered for 30 years and unravelled into three distinctly different threads: the exiles abroad, many of whom had left the country when they were too young to drive, the prisoners inside the jails, and the protestors throughout the country, who had never known a normal society. He had to knit these diverse factions of the anti-apartheid movement into something strong enough to withstand the intense pressures of further negotiations.

It takes a long time to organize an overnight miracle. For 14 long months, Mandela had been secretly, patiently negotiating with the enemy. That was just the beginning. It was obviously going to take a long time because his opponents still hadn't learnt from their mistakes and remained hugely frightened of black rule. Even now, moves were afoot to separate him from the ANC. He knew that the National Party had fatally underestimated him. They wanted a puppet, someone who would stand up and obediently read from a script that apartheid was dead while it still lived. What he didn't know was just how far the regime would go to cling on to power.

Some people expected talks to begin immediately and were disappointed that they did not. But while keeping the lines of communication open with his former jailers, Mandela outwitted his opponents by travelling extensively abroad in his first year of freedom, to keep sanctions in place so that the foot-dragging government would continue negotiating. Some critics accused him of forgetting his people at home, but Mandela was also wisely undertaking a ruthless round of fundraising to make sure that the liberation movements had the financial stamina to survive the long, hard rounds of give and take that awaited at the negotiating tables.

Everyone wanted a piece of Mandela magic. He coped graciously with many foreign individuals and governments who tried hard to take exclusive credit

Happy families? The Mandelas pose for the cameras a day after Nelson's Mandela's release.

At home with foreign dignitaries, Mandela chats with Pope John Paul II.

for his reappearance after so long in prison, and he didn't let the adulation go to his head; decades in prison had bled him dry of ego and left him with a clear perspective on the world. "I'm just a sinner who keeps on trying," he told people who tried to turn him into a saint.

Anthony Sampson, a long-term friend of Mandela's, summed it up beautifully: "Mandela's basic appeal was not as a man of power but as a moral leader who had stood out for fundamental principles and who gave hope for the future to all oppressed people and all countries torn by racial divisions." But the truth was that Mandela needed power in order to implement those fundamental principles. He had no vote, and many of the people who supported him were barred from voting as well. All he had to back him up in the fight for democracy were the twin threats of financial sanctions and a return to armed struggle, and the hope of his people.

The government was in no rush to enter into negotiations. They basked in the reflected glow of Mandela's release. Playing for time, the government chose to conduct a referendum among white voters only, still oblivious to the fact that this excluded millions of other adults from the process. Very little progress was made – and it gave resentful whites who thought they were being sold out by the government precious time to organize secret underground networks of violence and intimidation.

The high-ranking apartheid government ministers in their limousines and government houses had their hopes invested in Mandela. They saw him as their way out from endless civil war. But they also wanted him to cover their retreat from democracy; they remained wedded to the idea of group rights, not individual rights. Indeed, they were so accustomed to being in control that it was a shock when Mandela politely informed them that they were not allowed to have any say in who would be members of the first, historic, delegation of the ANC back to South Africa. Some of them were outraged: imagine, selecting your own delegation, they muttered. It was difficult to tell sometimes who was head of state: Mandela was polished, grave, funny, thoughtful and intelligent. The people who were

Cape Town rioting in the late 1980s. The violence continued well after Mandela's release.

actually in power dodged questions, complained, battled to give clear answers and often sounded more like red-handed schoolboys than statesmen. Mandela sounded like a president long before he actually became one.

Nearly two years after his release, Mandela finally saw the opening he'd been waiting for and negotiations commenced. In December, 228 delegates from 19 political parties joined the Convention for a Democratic South Africa. Almost every grouping attended, with the exception of some small right-wing Afrikaaner splinter groups with alarmingly close military ties. Another solitary holdout was Mangosuthu Buthelezi, a moody, erratic character who had thought that he would be the country's first black president while Mandela died in jail. Buthelezi had grown used to making his own decisions as a government-appointed leader of one of the pseudo-independent black homelands known as "kwaZulu" – "The place of the Zulu". The government promoted Buthelezi as the only alternative to Mandela possible, but found to their surprise that he was virtually uncontrollable. The Zulu chief sulked because he hadn't been allowed to bring three separate delegations to negotiations, and stalked out. He would continue to

play the role of spoiler for as long as possible, to the delight of conservative groups in Europe and America who saw Buthelezi as more biddable than the imposing, formidable Mandela. Violence in Buthelezi's former homeland dictatorship, kwaZulu, had already spilled out into the neighbouring province of Natal, and threatened the lives and property of nearly a quarter of the country's inhabitants. Soon it would go national.

The South African government did not play fair in negotiations – not that anyone expected them to. They used military power to try to spy out Mandela's strategies and block progress towards freedom. It became obvious that the government had absolutely no intention of abdicating power. Instead, government delegates kept suggesting detailed, convoluted, complicated compromises – American-style federal politics, Swiss-style canton politics, German-style states – anything but the simplicity of one person, one vote, one country. Their strategy was to hold on to as much power as possible, for as long as possible. Mandela's strategy, on the other hand, was to offer power to the people, and trust in them.

Mandela, who had been a champion stick-fighter in Transkei, dusted off his fighting skills. He had a

Left: A boy whipped by the South African police holds his fist up in defiance.

powerful team of people, trained in the long battle against apartheid, toughened by prison, polished in international diplomacy, and they soon outclassed the government negotiators. The unflappable Walter Sisulu, sounding like an Olympic coach or a sports commentator, assessed his old prison mate with a few, succinct words. "He's doing better than I expected," Sisulu said.

But that was inside the World Trade Centre, where what analysts called "the most spectacular negotiations of the century", were held just a taxi drive away from the Johannesburg airport. Outside, violence was being carefully orchestrated in a dirty tricks campaign to try to make Mandela appear helpless to control his own people, damage his reputation and force him into a corner.

Every month since Mandela walked free, at least 100 people died in politically motivated fighting in one region alone: the interlinked patchwork of

"Take your guns, your knives and your pangas and throw them into the sea!"

official Zulu-language homeland territory scattered throughout nominally white and Indian cities and towns of Natal on the country's east coast. Some commentators liked to present this as ethnic violence, as evidence that black South Africans were too tribally divided to govern themselves – but almost all the victims were Zulu speaking. Other analysts crudely dubbed the murders and house-burnings as "black on black violence", blithely ignoring the fact that one side – the conservative Inkatha party supporters led by Buthelezi – were working intimately with the white policemen and soldiers of the apartheid government. At Mandela's first big rally in this territory an ominous mutter swept through the crowd of supporters when he uttered the now-famous words, "Take your guns, your knives and your pangas [a type of sharp machete] and throw them into the sea!" Mandela, the crowd's hero, was in danger of being booed because the violence seemed unstoppable.

In other parts of the country, the crowded, single-sex hostels housing migrant workers from kwaZulu and Natal soon came under the control of Inkatha and the killings spread, triggering a vicious cycle of retaliation. The police force and the army simply stood by, claiming they were helpless. In 1990, Mandela himself had been tipped off in advance about trouble in Sebokeng, south of Johannesburg, when someone had mysteriously found the money to bring in busload after busload of armed hostel dwellers. He warned the government, who did nothing – and thirty ordinary people died, many deliberately mutilated and hacked by Inkatha supporters. The state's contempt for black lives nearly scuppered the early round of talks.

Many such massacres happened whenever a breakthrough seemed imminent. A thousand lives were lost in the month after Mandela signed the all-important Pretoria Minute agreement with the president. Mandela's own supporters began to feel that he could not protect them. The death toll far surpassed the killings during the apartheid era. The president who had released Mandela, F. W. de Klerk, liked to portray himself as weak and helpless. In one of many not-so-subtle requests for Mandela to abandon his insistence on full democracy and simply share power and title with him, de Klerk once said, "Mr Mandela, when you join me you will realize I do not have the power which you think I have."

This was the time of the shadowy third force. Killers roamed the trains from townships to towns, killing people and throwing bullet-ridden bodies off trains. Homeless refugees, the traumatized survivors of night-time raids by armed men, crowded churches and classrooms. Many young black men gave up on negotiations and armed themselves, blurring the line between politics and crime. Many young white men were forced to join the troops in the townships, or fled the country. From a time of hope, South Africa descended into bleak despair.

Mandela grew to distrust de Klerk, warning him repeatedly that the killers had to be coming from within his own government, from his own generals, his own policemen, his own soldiers. His warnings fell on deaf ears – until investigative journalists

"I FEEL LIKE AN OLD BATTERY THAT HAS BEEN RECHARGED!"

State-sponsored violence continues despite negotiations. On June 17, 1992, armed warriors singing in Zulu, and policemen with blackened faces leave Boipatong burning, and 45 dead.

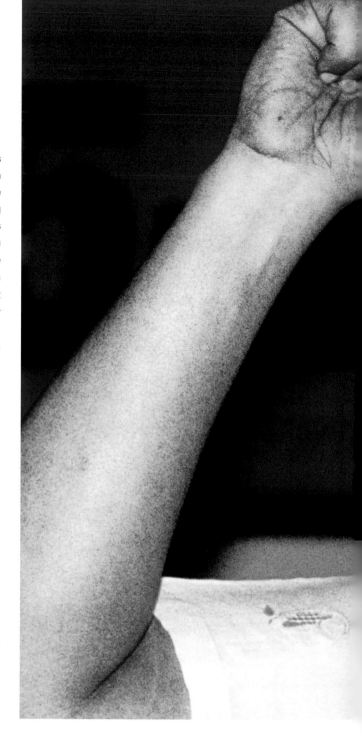

uncovered evidence that defense force soldiers were deliberately destabilizing the country with hit squads, using taxpayers' money. Still the government did nothing. Journalistic digging revealed that the South African taxpayer was subsidizing the so-called independent Zulu movement Inkatha, with the full knowledge of Mangosuthu Buthelezi, the so-called Teflon politician who claimed to oppose apartheid but who had never spent a day in jail or police custody in his life.

By 1992, negotiations deadlocked. Then on the winter evening of June 17, armed warriors waving Inkatha flags and singing Inkatha songs in Zulu, escorted by white policemen with blackened faces, openly moved into an ANC-supporting informal settlement not far from Johannesburg by the name of Boipatong. By the time they left, Boipatong was burning – and 45 people were dead.

Mandela broke off talks. Heartsick and tired of pleading for peace from the paralysed government, he visited Boipatong and attended the mass funeral of the victims. "Give us guns," people pleaded with him in desperation. "Kill the Boers." For the next three months, it seemed like war had returned to almost every South African street. At the end of this time, tens of thousands of marchers moved into one of the other so-called homelands established under apartheid to house black citizens. But the collaborators who ran the small, poverty-stricken Ciskei homeland staked their future on the survival of apartheid and the endurance of the white government. Soldiers opened fire without warning and killed 28 protestors, many of them in the back.

It was the shock that Mandela used to pull the nation back from the brink of full-scale war. One massacre had driven him away from the negotiating tables; another massacre showed everyone involved that they had to return. There were no other options, he pointed out. An astounding series of 40 meetings happened quietly, through quiet back channels of communication. Multiparty negotiations resumed at the beginning of 1993.

But the government balked at many issues, including the release of all political prisoners, regardless of what they had been convicted for.

They also objected to fencing off the hostile hostels and banning the murderous traditional weapons used by vigilantes. The white government caved in and signed the pivotal Record of Understanding. It agreed on a joint coalition to govern South Africa, a transitional government of national unity in which virtually any party could participate, and a constitutional assembly in which no one would be barred. Mandela in turn protected the jobs and pensions of the bloated bureaucracy of the white civil service and made many other expensive compromises. South Africa had come a huge step closer to election day.

Buthelezi, ever the spoiler, pulled out. Although the government claimed never to be in control of the third force, the train attacks dwindled. Massacres were fewer, although high-profile incidents of violence continued. The government seemed to accept the inevitability of losing power, because it dismantled its seven secret nuclear bombs – perhaps fearing what might happen when someone else had their finger on the trigger.

It was a sign of progress but once again, disaster struck. On April 10, 1993, the hugely popular and bright Chris Hani, former commander of the armed wing of the ANC, was assassinated in the driveway of his home, in front of his teenage daughter. The charismatic Hani was one of the most militant soldiers under Mandela's command, and had only just recently come to accept the need for negotiations. South Africa seemed poised to return to the cycle of violence, which it knew so well.

"I thought Chris was going to bury me," mourned Mandela's Oliver Tambo. "Not me bury Chris." Another shadowy third force hit? But luck stepped in. A white, Afrikaans-speaking woman happened to note down the licence plate of a car speeding away, and the police arrested a Polish immigrant,

Chris Hani, a hugely popular figure, fearlessly championed the cause of freedom and equality in South Africa.

"I FEEL LIKE AN OLD BATTERY THAT HAS BEEN RECHARGED!"

full of hate towards communists, and a foppish member of the whites-only, deeply racist Conservative Party of South Africa. At least two members of the third force had been identified.

Mandela forced national television to broadcast his appeal for peace. A grief-stricken nation listened. Seventy people died in the Hani riots but a full-scale bloodbath did not happen. Hani's murder would take one more victim: Oliver Tambo, already weakened by a stroke, left Hani's graveside coughing up dust. Within a fortnight, the old man who had launched the Free Mandela campaign around the world was dead. "Perhaps I shall not live to see the Promised Land," he once told his wife Adelaide. "But my people shall have reached it."

Hani's murder and Tambo's passing fresh in his mind, Mandela returned to the negotiating table with a clear order to his lieutenants: set a date for an election. Tambo and Hani had not lived to cast a vote. Mandela was determined to do it for them. His opponents stalled, pointing out that the country lacked a constitution. He insisted on a date. The time for prevaricating while people died was over.

Two months later, most of the parties agreed to hold South Africa's first ever genuine elections. "The countdown to the democratic transfer of power to the people has begun," Mandela announced. The date was set: April 27, 1994.

But it looked as though his old rival Mangosuthu Buthelezi was going to do more than boycott the election; he was trying to secede. Twenty people, including schoolchildren, were massacred in territory under his control near the provincial capital of Pietermaritzburg. Three thousand Afrikaans-speaking protestors, wearing army-style uniforms and carrying a flag similar to the Nazi swastika, invaded negotiations and urinated in front of the delegates while shouting racist insults, trying to provoke war. Five radical young men, all black, rushed into a church in Cape Town, killing 11 members of the mostly white congregation and injuring many more. Pull out, pull out, urged protestors. But Mandela had studied enough history to know that this was exactly what the perpetrators wanted him to do. He stuck to negotiations.

In Mandela's personal life, negotiations were a complete and utter failure. In 1992, a grim-faced and physically tense Mandela reluctantly announced his separation from Winnie. For a man who preferred to keep his emotional life out of the newspapers, it was a deeply humiliating day. "Ladies and gentlemen," he told the media slowly, "I hope you appreciate the pain I have gone through."

Mandela was loyal to a fault. But the tensions with his headstrong, wayward spouse, who was constantly in trouble with their own liberation movement for inciting the youngsters to violence, whose dubious taste in friends led to accusations of infiltrators and corruption, whose financial dealings were unsavoury, irresponsible and even fraudulent,

> Tambo and Hani had not lived to cast a vote. Mandela was determined to do it for them.

had been looming for years. Oliver Tambo's diary as long ago as 1989, when Mandela was still in jail, noted, "Nel poised to seek divorce."

Even during the announcement, Mandela graciously paid tribute to his wife's contribution to the struggle. Winnie was Mandela's lifeline when he was in prison. She suffered greatly for it, including torture.

She was fearless and physically unafraid. But the victim of violence was herself prone to outbreaks of shouting and apparently the occasional use of her fists, and heavy drinking. Her husband remained a teetotaller, writing off the stories he heard about his wife as anti-apartheid propaganda.

Winnie also began a pattern of financial chaos, running up large and extravagant bills, falling into debt, and unable to explain why cheques meant for the struggle seemed to evaporate. In the 1980s, she was consorting with American lawyers to capitalize on the Mandela brand. While her husband

April 1993: The country hovers on the brink of civil war following the assassination of ANC leader Chris Hani. Mandela appears on television urging restraint.

was able to squash that initiative from inside his jail cell, he would not learn of others until it was too late. Many friends worried that prison, isolation and torture had damaged her beyond repair – but most people never raised their fears, because they didn't want to damage her reputation at a time when she was the sole voice of Mandela.

In prison, Mandela wrote her letters charged with sexual longing and infused with erotic imagery, in defiance of the ever-present censors. In a similar fashion, the international media loved her: beautiful and wide-eyed, energetic and well-dressed, sexy, fiery, always ready with a good quote. The press helped turn her into an American idol, a monster who believed her own propaganda as "mother of the nation", who was above anybody's law. But the media would turn on her with a vengeance.

Fully outfitted in glamorous military style from her feet to her headgear, she began to incite the youth to violence, which put Mandela's old friend Oliver Tambo in a terrible position. The liberation movement needed unity in the fight against apartheid, so Tambo felt that he could not criticize Mandela's wife openly. Privately he asked her to keep quiet. She did not. She played to the crowds, crowing that the barbaric necklacing method of murdering opponents by placing a petrol-filled tyre around their necks – and igniting it – would burn

open a path of liberation. Her comments delighted the apartheid government, who refused to act against her. But her shocked husband would not act against his beloved wife – certainly not while he was in prison and didn't have access to all the facts.

Soon Winnie would embark on more extreme violence in Soweto with the Mandela Football Club and her personal team of bodyguards. Several members had faced kidnapping and murder charges. Some were spies. In those lawless times, the Mandela Football Club, operating openly in the township, became one of many vigilante squads. Mandela ordered his wilful wife to disband it. She refused, creating the kind of stress and division within the movement that even the police force and army had not been able to achieve. Before, she had been Mandela's wife. Now, she was someone in her own right. She was the sole voice of the struggle. And she was completely out of control.

In a turf war between his wife's bodyguards and a rival group of thugs, Mandela's home, with all his irreplaceable photographs, letters and notes, was burnt down in 1988. He was devastated by the loss of his family history. Another attempt was made at getting the football club disbanded. It wasn't. Eventually the respected Truth and Reconciliation Commission (TRC), established in post-apartheid South Africa by Mandela to find out the truth about

Mandela set up the Truth and Reconciliation Commission under Anglican Archbishop Desmond Tutu to uncover the truth about lies and atrocities committed during the fight against apartheid. Here, Winnie appears before the Commission.

Left: Winnie delivers a speech at a meeting in Umtata, the former Transkei. Mandela's wife suffered greatly from imprisonment and torture, but later became out of control.

Gary Kruser describes to the Truth and Reconciliation Commission how policemen pinned his arms behind his head and tortured him when he was captured as an ANC guerrilla in the 1980s.

these troubled times, would hold his former wife personally responsible for the brutal deaths of two local young activists, Lolo Sono and his friend Sibuniso Tshabalala, accused of being informers. But the TRC had no power to dish out punishment, so she went on, unscathed.

In 1988 Winnie was the Queen of Soweto, and resented any curbs on her power. A Methodist minister who provided help for local boys on the run fell victim to her smear campaign falsely alleging that he was a homosexual child abuser. Her team of bodyguards kidnapped some of the young

men and she reportedly watched as they were brutally beaten and interrogated. The body of one of them, 14-year-old Stompie Seipei, was found in a riverbed. When activists tried to reign in her behaviour, she broke with the movement's longstanding commitment to a multiracial society, spouting xenophobic words of hate. "We are not prepared to remain silent where those who are violating human rights claim to be doing so in the name of the struggle against apartheid," was the devastating response from her own friends, a group of respected leaders who formed the Mandela

Crisis Committee. She had gone too far. The citizens of Soweto threatened to revolt against her.

Winnie herself always blamed others for the trouble she found herself in. In 1991, when she was on trial for the kidnap and assault of Stompie Seipei, she said it was "police harassment". Mandela, desperately busy with talks, found that he had to take away precious time to support his wife in court. She didn't pay for her own lawyers and well-meaning funders from Sweden and other countries eventually paid the bill in the mistaken belief that this was political persecution. The court case was hampered by missing witnesses and alibi-destroying material withheld by the security police, who may have been hoping to blackmail the future first lady. Nonetheless, the judge found Mandela's wife to be "a calm, composed, deliberate and unblushing liar". She was sentenced to six years in jail, reduced on appeal to a fine and a suspended sentence.

Even later, when her behaviour was scrutinized by the post-apartheid Truth and Reconciliation Commission led by the much-loved Nobel Peace Prize-winning minister Desmond Tutu, she accused the investigators of conspiracies and bias. If anything, the reverse seems to be true: hardly anybody in the legal fraternity dared touch her.

"Together in their separation," was how a friend wisely diagnosed the relationship between husband and wife. "In their togetherness they began to discover how apart they had become."

After Mandela's release, Winnie cooked meals, and welcomed old friends. It was a façade. Winnie didn't want to be a domestic goddess. She wanted to be a power in her own right. And she was not prepared to relinquish the partners she had turned to in the lonely times of Mandela's jail sentence. They kept almost completely different hours in the same house, with reports of him rising early to prepare for negotiations and her staggering home in the wee hours of the night, sometimes even needing help to get into a bed. Mandela was torn. Old friends who warned him against his wife could find themselves thoroughly snubbed. But the man who could talk to his jailers found himself unable to talk with his wife.

Because of her high profile overseas, well-meaning but naïve friends pushed for Winnie to have a recognizable position. The former social worker was made head of the ANC welfare department in 1994, to the private dismay of many. Mandela asked for her finances to be investigated when funds went missing but at the same time he also asked journalists not to print damaging articles. Eventually, some of the truth leaked out. Winnie had cashed welfare donations in the name of one of her lovers. This triggered the separation.

Winnie never gave up hope of reconciliation and Mandela was torn by his loyalty to the mother of his children. Later she became a Member of Parliament:

> ... with preparations for an election well under way, it was announced that the Nobel Peace Prize would be jointly awarded to both Mandela and the man who had let him out of jail, South African president Frederik Willem de Klerk.

a Deputy Minister of Arts. But she was criticized for not attending parliament and ignoring her responsibilities. Instead, she became involved in an astonishing series of shady deals: diamond deals, twisted tourist programmes, anti-poverty wars with fat expense accounts and housing fraud.

In 1993, with preparations for an election well under way, it was announced that the Nobel Peace Prize would be jointly awarded to both Mandela and the man who had let him out of jail, South African president Frederik Willem de Klerk.

The two opponents, wary and exhausted, both facing the collapse of their marriages, flew to Norway, to accept their prizes. But Mandela's heart was sore. And there were many more crises to be fixed before he could, for the first time in his long life, cast a piece of paper into a box and say, "I have cast my vote."

The two past adversaries share
the Nobel Peace Prize stage, Oslo,
Norway, 1993.

CHAPTER 9

President Nelson Mandela

In April 1994, for the first time in South Africa's history, all races voted in democratic elections, and Mandela was elected the country's first black President. Over the next five years, he strove to create a new image for South Africa while dealing with domestic issues such as housing and poverty. On his 80th birthday he married Graça Machel, widow of Mozambique's President.

For three days, the lines snaked across the country. In the suburbs, maids and madams, oppressor and victim, policeman and gangster, employer and unemployed, farmers and farmhands, waited patiently for the chance to vote. In the rural areas, vast crocodiles of people curved back and forth outside schools and churches that had been hastily transformed into voting stations. Elderly men who couldn't walk made their grandsons take them in wheelbarrows. A determined crippled woman crawled from her rural home over several kilometres of dirt path to her voting station. Heavily pregnant women were waved to the front of the line by smiling people who had been waiting since before sunrise. It was as if 23 million voters were enjoying themselves at a slightly chaotic party.

The voting was spread over three days in order to cope with inexperience and shortages and attempts to disrupt the voting. International monitors and bloodthirsty journalists went away disappointed. True, there were bombs from right-wing Afrikaans groups in the run-up to the election, killing 20, in a last-ditch effort to get a pure white, Afrikaans-speaking homeland territory of their own. It was not a peaceful time.

In addition, there had been considerable violence in a number of the nominally independent black homelands of Ciskei, Bophutatswana (or Bop), and kwaZulu. But Bop soldiers had turned on aggressive armed right-wingers called in by their own dictator, and shot some dead in front of television cameras. The aging Bop dictator, Lucas Mangope, then agreed to allow his people to participate in the election. The Ciskei crumbled. And at the last moment, Mangosuthu Buthelezi dropped his threats of pulling kwaZulu out of the country and agreed to participate in the elections instead of calling for yet another postponement.

> ... maids and madams, oppressor and victim, policeman and gangster, employer and unemployed, farmers and farmhands, waited patiently for the chance to vote.

This was a relief for Mandela but a nerve-wracking occurrence for the election organizers, who quickly had to stick millions of additions on to the ballot paper. With dozens of obscure special interest groups and homeland parties registered, the ballot paper was a long sheet of paper, with each party's name in English, symbol and the photograph of its leader listed next to the box waiting to be ticked. The photograph and the symbol were to assist South Africa's many illiterate voters and voters not fluent in English. Mandela, three-quarters of a century old, used to joke with audiences, telling them to run down the list of leaders until they came

Mandela marries his third wife, Graça Machel, on his 80th birthday.

Following page:
For three days, the voting lines snaked across the country. Here, hundreds of people wait to vote in Mandela's home village.

NELSON MANDELA

A 75-year-old invalid from a squatter camp outside Cape Town is helped to cast his vote.

to him: "When you see the face of a young and handsome man, mark X."

Overseas analysts flew in to comfortable hotel rooms, where they stayed, with many of the pundits predicting anarchy after the elections, accusing people like Mandela of promising voters the world. But television footage showed the opposite. "Do not expect to be driving a Mercedes the day after the election or swimming in your own backyard pool," Mandela repeatedly warned people on the brink of voting for the first time. "Life will not change dramatically, except that you will have increased your self-esteem and become a citizen in your own land. You must have patience." Indeed, often Mandela sounded more like a schoolmaster, instructing students who had fought in self-defence units that they would have to go back to school, and warning people not to heed the seductive call of the shebeens, the thriving, illegal drinking establishments that had sprung up in many township. "We cannot do it all for you," Mandela tells the voters. "You must do it yourselves."

So in 1994, at the grand old age of 75, a beaming Nelson Mandela cast his first vote in a wooden box in a high school in a Durban township:

a region torn apart for years by vicious fighting. It could have been civil war. Instead, it was so peaceful that some monitors complained of being bored. A journalist called out as Mandela entered the polling station to ask who he was voting for. Mandela laughed. "You know," he teased, "I have been agonizing over that choice all morning."

It took several anxious days to collect the ballot boxes from isolated settlements and count them in front of jittery and suspicious witnesses. The results showed a huge wave of support for Mandela and his party, an overwhelming sign that people agreed with negotiations over war, opening the way to form a true government of national unity. Mandela was delighted in a way that two provinces chose not to elect ANC rulers in this first historic election. One was kwaZulu-Natal, which incorporated both the apartheid-era Zulu homeland and the white and Indian farms and cities dating back to colonial time, which voted for his old rival Mangosuthu Buthelezi's Zulu nationalist party Inkatha. The other was the Western Cape, historically home to much of the so-called coloured or mixed race population, which had often felt itself squeezed between black resentment and white resistance. But because

Deputy President Thabo Mbeki, the exiled son of Mandela's old revolutionary colleague Govan Mbeki, is pictured addressing ANC supporters in 1999.

Mandela's party, the ANC, did not have a two-thirds majority, it would not be able to write its own constitution. It would have to continue negotiations. Mandela believed this would be the best thing for the country in the long run. "I am your servant," he said in his victory speech, his voice hoarse with a cold. "This is a time to heal the old wounds and build a new South Africa."

"I saw my mission as one of preaching reconciliation," Mandela later wrote. He appointed the man who took him out of jail, his old enemy at the negotiating table, F. W. de Klerk, as the First Deputy President of a free South Africa. The Second Deputy President was a pipe-smoking intellectual 25 years younger than his boss, Thabo Mbeki, the exiled son of Mandela's old revolutionary

May 10, 1994. Mandela is sworn in as the country's first ever black president.

colleague Govan Mbeki, the only person accurately to predict disaster when the headstrong and overconfident young Mandela came out of hiding.

Rebuilding a nation was immensely difficult, lonely work. His soulmate Oliver Tambo was dead, and his lifelong mentor Walter Sisulu chose not to be in the first cabinet, preferring to continue his role as a quiet backroom power broker and strategist. Their relationship was strong enough that he could

be a curb on Mandela's occasional tendency to play the role of chief, and Sisulu was clearly watching for any signs that success was going to Mandela's head. He was reassured, saying, "I have no fears that you're going to have a dictator arising from him." The first multiracial cabinet reflected the stresses of the country but was able to work well nonetheless – for a time.

But Sisulu's withdrawal and Tambo's death meant

South Africans, and an astonishing one billion people watching the broadcast live on television, he cut a solitary figure. His daughter was half-hidden under a large black hat, more suitable for a funeral than a day of rejoicing.

His first ex-wife, Evelyn Mase, reluctantly allowed at the time of voting that perhaps she would not have ever had this opportunity if it hadn't been for the man she had divorced because of his obsession with freedom. She was not invited to the inauguration. His second wife, Winnie Madikizela Mandela, sat in the audience that day in an enormous green hat, which obscured the view of people behind her, but her presence was not a sign of tolerance or truce. This was the woman who never changed her radical stance, describing her former husband's Nobel Peace Prize as a bribe, an award for selling out the country in negotiations. Despite this, she was still lobbying for a reconciliation with her spouse, who showed no sign of rushing for divorce. But she did it in a way designed to hurt and wound her husband: she asked her old flame Kaizer Matanzima, the discredited leader who had collaborated with the white regime and had long tried to corrupt and bribe Mandela, to negotiate on her behalf. Mandela was outraged, and refused.

At that historic ceremony in which Mandela became president, he didn't smile much, even when the military – at a time when nobody knew how loyal the old generals would be to their new leaders – executed a dazzling pinpoint swoop of jets, helicopters and troop carriers low over the crowd, staking their allegiance to the new order. Perhaps he was lonely. Perhaps the former terrorist and jailbird was simply conscious of the heavy weight of history: "We, who were outlaws not so long ago, have today been given the rare privilege to be host to the nations of the world on our own soil," he noted in his acceptance speech. This was not boasting. South Africa had been so isolated by years of boycotts in virtually all spheres of life – universities, the arts, sports, industry, trade and finance – that this was the first and biggest gathering of international faces in the country. Mandela had claimed his birthright, and in doing so returned South Africa – once a

that Mandela had lost his two closest friends. He had deeply strained relationships with two ex-wives, with four surviving children, and even with his grandchildren. Even though his eldest daughter from his second marriage, Zenani, now a Swazi princess in the last absolute monarchy in Africa, accompanied him to the swearing-in ceremony, with thousands crowding the Union Buildings in Pretoria, which had once been off-limits to black global outcast itself – back into the embrace of a waiting world. He would always retain an almost childlike glee at meeting famous people and celebrities.

South Africans rejoiced at the end of long years of isolation. Athletes began training for the Olympics for the first time, while rugby, cricket and soccer teams were given their first chance to compete against the world. Audiences found themselves on the touring schedules of musicians and performers. Scientists and researchers were able to attend overseas conferences, and bring world-class leaders back to their own students. But the end of isolation for the country was also a terribly isolating time for Mandela.

Mandela would always retain a childlike glee at meeting celebrities. American talk show personality Oprah Winfrey donates 10 million US dollars from her foundation for an academy for girls in Johannesburg.

As a leader, his focus was on preserving the tenuous peace, so fragile, so easily destroyed. He focused on reconciliation between races, sometimes to the impatience of colleagues who also wanted to focus on ways to compensate people for the incredible damage wrought by apartheid. The challenge facing South Africa, he often pointed out, is not just between the black majority and the white minority but it is also how to narrow the divide between the rich and the poor. Nation-building and reconciliation between races may have been the hallmark of Mandela's presidency, but poverty was also an important priority.

In the meantime, there were many practical difficulties. He returned to the government rooms where he had once been a prisoner pleading for negotiations to begin. He had to spend precious time reassuring his civil servants that they were not going to be thrown out on the streets, while his staff tried to work out where keys were and why documents were missing and why the computer

French President François Mitterand meets Mandela in Cape Town, 1994.

systems wouldn't communicate with each other. (It turned out that racial segregation extended even to information technology, so that computers dealing with black orphans at the Department of Welfare, for example, were incompatible with the government computers used to store information about prospective white parents.)

Progress and change came slowly to the Rainbow Nation. Rural people began to receive clean water, telephone lines and postal services which linked them to the rest of the world. Schools and clinics were built – although it was sometimes difficult to find staff to fill them. Houses – not always of the best quality – were quickly built in the regions where the homeless congregated, leading to accusations that the government wasn't doing enough to overturn the legacy of segregation.

The French leader François Mitterand, whose wife had quietly done much to bring the two sides together, became the first foreign head of state to speak within the walls of the 84-year-old parliament since British Prime Minister Harold Macmillan in 1960. "You are building a new nation," Mitterand told the 490 black and white legislators. "My ambition is that France should be by your side."

Many other leaders came offering help, but much of it was accompanied by conditions which made it difficult to accept. The government realized that it was not going to receive much international help, and would have to find the money itself. In addition, the world had changed. Mandela had been put into jail by a powerful nation, which could somehow survive the hostility of the rest of the world. He was now a president in a world which had shrunk. Powerful multinational companies shunned the new democratic South Africa, and the state was no

Queen Elizabeth II visits Mandela and South Africa in 1995.

ANC exile Albie Sachs lost the sight in one eye and the use of an arm after being the victim of a South African car bomb in Mozambique. Sachs is now a Justice of the Constitutional Court of South Africa.

longer able to go it alone. There were limits to his power regardless of how many people had voted for him.

There was worse. Mandela discovered to his shock that the previous government, led by the man who was now his deputy president, had deliberately caused enormous harm to both the national economy and his project of nation-building. The country was virtually bankrupt. He was going to have to transform the face of South Africa with almost no money in the treasury and little or no help from abroad. Enormous loans had been taken out on the eve of the transfer of power, and he was now responsible for honouring those apartheid-era obligations. Just before the election, the outgoing government had unilaterally given thousands of policemen secret indemnity from prosecution for any crimes they committed during apartheid. Mandela could not overturn it. He had told people to be patient, to wait five years. Now it seemed that he might not see improvements in the lives of his people before the next election. And the numbers of unemployed people, especially amongst the impatient young adults, rose higher and higher. The new government could offer them little: there was almost no money for welfare, unemployment insurance was riddled with fraud, and there was no cash for training. What money there was had already been sucked up to protect the jobs and pensions of the existing white civil servants during

negotiations – and Mandela was not the type of man to go back on his word.

He did not ever give up. One of Mandela's most important achievements was the final creation of a new constitution. It will stand as a lasting legacy to his far-sighted vision when he is finally at rest. It is a constitution that will shape the country for decades, regardless of who rules it, protecting the people from the worst excesses of politics even though it outrages many people at the same time. The constitution outlaws the death penalty, permits abortion, and refuses almost any kind of discrimination – black or white, male or female, homosexual or heterosexual, rich or poor. The echoes of the past struggles can be heard in the constitution, widely considered one of the best in the world. Indeed, the first constitutional court was chaired by a lawyer who as a young and compassionate professional 30 years earlier had helped defend Mandela and his comrades in the Rivonia Trial.

When Mandela formally opened the court in 1995, he reminded people that the last time he had been in court, it was to find out if he was going to be hung for the crime of demanding freedom for his people. Later, he would make a point of having lunch with the once-vindictive prosecutor – now a small and frail man– who had tried to have him hung by the neck in the same trial. He hunted down almost all the powerful people who had tried to hurt or betray the struggle. And then he hugged them. Many of his own friends balked at his acts of

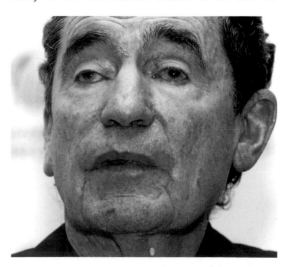

forgiveness, interpreting them as a chance for people to dodge the consequences of their own evil behaviour – but Mandela, the sunny optimist, saw it differently. "Courageous people do not fear forgiving," he told one critic.

Mandela himself lived frugally, donating a third of his salary to the Nelson Mandela Children's Fund. He was hurt when some of his colleagues – often activists who were being pressured by irresponsible members of their own, poverty-stricken extended families – were found to behave in unethical and even fraudulent ways. It was a time when many people wanted some kind of financial reward for

the long years of struggle and hardship. Mandela found himself torn between loyalty and integrity, between activists' past heroics and present unscrupulous excesses, many, many times. As with his abusers, he found it easier to forgive than to demand redress.

He did institute another world-changing first: the Truth and Reconciliation Commission, a way to forgive without forgetting. In 1996, the Truth Commission lifted the carpet of secrecy, and in public meetings around the nation began to sweep out the hidden stories of murder, rape, torture, assault, theft, homelessness and destruction which

Anglican Archbishop Desmond Tutu and fellow commissioners listen to testimony at the start of the Truth and Reconciliation Commission. Even ANC members were called to account for their actions: "Yesterday's oppressed can quite easily become today's oppressors," Tutu warned.

made up the lives of many people under apartheid. It was a brutal, painful spring-cleaning for the entire nation, and it was not without its critics. If the policemen, soldiers, ministers, vigilantes and rebels did not tell the truth, they could face prosecution in court. Prosecution was an unlikely prospect, however, because so much of the paperwork had been destroyed by the outgoing government. The dead could tell no tales, and both the victims and the perpetrators were getting old. The chances of tracing the chain of command to the highest level in the land were slim.

The Truth Commission was never meant to be a court of justice or a Nuremberg-style war crimes trial aimed at executing the ringleaders. It was about getting the true stories out into the harsh daylight, so that the killers could ease their troubled souls, so that their victims could confront their abusers, and so that white South Africans could no longer say that they did not know what atrocities had been committed in their name. At the very least, some families learnt about the last moments of missing sons and daughters, and were sometimes able to collect the bones and have a formal farewell. Even

ANC leaders, sometimes to their surprise, were called to account for their behaviour at the Truth and Reconciliation Commission and found themselves trying to take it to court. "Yesterday's oppressed can quite easily become today's oppressors," warned the Truth Commission's leader, Anglican Archbishop Desmond Tutu. With all its flaws, the Truth and Reconciliation Commission has since become a model for many other troubled nations around the world. Mandela may not have been able to achieve everything he wanted to as president, but he was still able to change the world, one step at a time.

In his long walk to freedom, Mandela found help and support from an unexpected quarter just before he was about to retire from active politics. In 1998, on his 80th birthday, Mandela became a newlywed. This time he married the lively Graça Machel, nearly 30 years younger, his long-term companion and an extraordinary intellect, parent and politician in her own right.

Mandela has always been interested in powerful women. Machel may be the most powerful of the lot – the First Lady of two different countries, a trained

The newlywed politician. At first Machel would not marry Mandela: "I belong to Mozambique," she declared. She finally accepted when a compromise was met: she would spend half her time in Mozambique and half in South Africa.

soldier just like both her husbands, and now an international stateswoman.

In Mozambique, a southern African colony brutally controlled by a long-running Portuguese dictatorship, Machel fled the Portuguese police after high school, to other parts of Europe, where she joined the independence movement known as the Front for the Liberation of Mozambique.

Like Mandela's Mkhonto we Sizwe soldiers, she ended up at a military training camp in Tanzania, where her main responsibility was to provide education for refugees. Eventually, she met the charismatic commander who was the equivalent of Mandela in Mozambique: Samora Machel. They married in 1975, the year that Mozambique finally gained independence from its Portuguese masters.

Graça Machel was a tower of strength: the powerful Minister of Education who slashed the country's illiteracy rate dramatically. But she gave up her job and mourned for years when Machel died in a plane crash in 1986 in the mountains separating Mozambique from the eastern border of South Africa. Many thought the plane crash was no accident, but another example of the apartheid government showing how far its military tentacles could stretch. Others blamed pilot and instrument failure.

Mandela was then in prison but was allowed by the prison censors to send her a touching note of condolence, which she thanked him for in a return letter. "From within your vast prison, you brought a ray of light in my hour of darkness," she noted.

They met in Mozambique after he was freed from prison, when some observers thought he flirted with her, but then Mandela flirted with many pretty women, and Graça Machel was still grieving. She was also deeply involved in campaigning for human rights, especially promoting the needs of young children.

Later, when Oliver Tambo died during negotiations, Mandela found he had inherited Tambo's responsibility as godfather to Machel's many children. The two gradually grew closer in the years following Mandela's painful separation from Winnie.

Winnie hadn't quite given up hopes of a reconciliation, and was scathing – even crudely ethnic – about "that Portuguese woman" and "the concubine". She accused Mandela of behaving in a

Mozambican soldiers carry away the coffin of Samora Machel from the aircraft wreckage where he died. The cause of the crash remains a mystery.

NELSON MANDELA

way that would damage his children emotionally, although they were all grown up and some even had grandchildren of their own. In a slightly embarrassing episode, both his first wife, Evelyn Mase, and his second spouse, claimed that in the eyes of God and according to traditional customary law, he remained their husband. It was beginning to sound as if, according to his former wives, Mandela had returned to his father's polygamous roots in his old age.

But Machel was against marriage. She thought it would be wrong to marry Mandela while he remained head of South Africa. "I belong to Mozambique," she declared. "I will always be the wife of Samora Machel."

Mandela was unable to persuade her otherwise. "She has made a clear statement that she will not marry the President of South Africa," he said somewhat ruefully. "I cannot overrule her."

Their compromise: she would spend half the month in the diplomatic quarters in the Mozambican seaside capital of Maputo, and cohabit half the month with him in Johannesburg. The press hounded the couple with constant intrusive questions as to when the couple would marry. "It is not something you discuss with journalists," was often Mandela's easy answer.

But it was pressure from friends – including another South African winner of the Nobel Peace Prize, the veteran anti-apartheid campaigner and bouncy, jovial Anglican Archbishop Desmond Tutu – that pushed the public relationship on to a more formal level, just six months before he was due to leave the presidency.

"People like Archbishop Tutu are making my life very difficult," Mandela complained. They quietly married in a service blessed by Jewish, Hindu, Muslim and Christian religious leaders (including Tutu) on Mandela's birthday. Having brought the country to its own peace, having united black and white, Mandela himself was at last personally happy. The struggle for personal joy may have taken longer than the struggle for freedom, but his sense of humour remained undimmed. One of the first things Mandela did after getting married was to turn to Tutu and cheerfully tell him, "Now you won't shout at me!"

Desmond Tutu collects his Nobel Peace Prize from chairman Egil Aarvik in Oslo, Norway, 1984.

CHAPTER 10

"I Can't Rest"

Children have been one of the great joys of Mandela's life since his release from prison, but relationships with his own offspring have been occasionally tense and full of unspoken sorrows. His stepchildren, grandchildren and now his great-grandchildren are less marked by history. But all children are special to him. The tall, stooped man with the bad knee will always interrupt his packed schedule to bend down and talk to a passing child.

AIDS, however, has attacked the generation known as the born-free: the young adults meant to be the main beneficiaries of Mandela's freedom. Apartheid destroyed generations, with the poorest particularly vulnerable to its evils. The virus is doing the same. The critical difference is that there was a strong, unified front against apartheid: even when people disagreed on tactics, they agreed on racism as the source of the problem. But the battle against AIDS is fragmented, with doctors pitted against politicians, husband against wife, church against condom, and so on. There remain people in South Africa who deny the very existence of the disease – and some of these people occupy some of the highest elected offices in the land.

Mandela's family is not immune to this deadly enemy. By 2005, at least four members of Mandela's extended family were known to have succumbed to AIDS. Most people are reluctant to reveal that their friends or family have died of the virus but Mandela did not mince words about his own family's deaths. On a visit to his roots in Transkei, Mandela became aware of the plight of a 22-year-old niece, and offered money to his half-brother for treatment. He was too late. "A few days after I got back to Johannesburg, I heard that she had died," he told journalists.

A well-to-do nephew in the same region lost two HIV-positive sons. The nature of their illness was kept from Mandela until, again, it was too late. But the AIDS stigma bedevils even this prominent family. Mandela, the man who could negotiate with jailers and murderers, asked for permission from his family to disclose the names of the two young men, "but

> The tall, stooped man with the bad knee will always interrupt his packed schedule to bend down and talk to a passing child.

they were not happy about that, so we can't disclose their identity".

Nor was he able to say if the young men had access to life-prolonging medication – a controversial issue in South Africa. Mandela's successor, president Thabo Mbeki, claims not to know anyone with AIDS and the Health Department has lashed out over criticism that it has not responded quickly enough to supply AIDS medication for the poor.

The older generation bridging the gap between the born-free and the struggle stalwarts is not

Mandela meets his grandchildren at their home in Soweto. Mandela always has time for children after the decades in prison when he couldn't see any.

Mandela, with wife Graça, attends the funeral of his last surviving son. Makgatho, who worked as a lawyer in the healthcare industry, died of AIDS in January 2005.

immune, either. Mandela's last remaining son, Makgatho, a quiet-spoken man who became a lawyer after his father left prison, died of AIDS in 2005. Makgatho's wife died a year earlier, possibly from AIDS-related pneumonia. Prison took Mandela away from his children. He did not expect AIDS to take his children away from him in his freedom.

Mandela has used his private pain for the greater good. As he announced the cause of his son's death, the 86-year-old former president pleaded with the nation in his distinctive, gravelly voice: "Let us give publicity to HIV/AIDS and not hide it, because [that is] the only way to make it appear like a normal illness." Even old enemies like the former Zulu homeland leader Mangosuthu Buthelezi – who had also announced the death of his own children from AIDS – praised his honesty and bravery.

Nonetheless, the virus is tearing through the country, killing more people than ever died in the struggle for freedom, causing untold economic havoc at a time meant for rebuilding, and leaving behind a generation of orphans. About a quarter of all adults are thought to be infected. Speaking at the 14th International AIDS Conference in Paris in 2003, before his own personal tragedies had happened, Mandela said that a "tragedy of unprecedented proportions" was unfolding in Africa. It is not the legacy he was hoping to leave behind.

When retiring as president, Mandela said that he looked forward to walking the hills and valleys of his home village in peace and tranquillity. "Don't call me, I'll call you," he joked to a world still eager to have a taste of Madiba magic. But the hills and valleys of his home village are now dotted with gravesites. Once again, he was forced to speak out. "What I want to stress is the devastating effect of AIDS on this country," Mandela told the world. "All of us have to stand up and make sure that this matter is widely publicized."

While many prominent political leaders have tried to minimize the impact of AIDS, with some descending into conspiracy theories and wild claims about unproven treatments, Mandela took refuge in a practical response. He pointed out that the extent of the epidemic, even though it is difficult to trace, was evident from the obituary columns of daily

newspapers such as Johannesburg's *The Sowetan*: "There was a time when obituaries covered only a small part of a page. Now it is two pages. If you look closely, you will see how serious the pandemic is."

Once again, he uses his presence and his publicity to raise money for a good cause. "We must be supportive of our relatives and encourage them by all means not to lose hope," he tells the press. "The determination to live is as important as the medicines prescribed by the doctors. We must encourage our relatives who are HIV-positive to disclose their status so they can be helped and attended to."

It has been a peculiar way to spend his retirement and what time remains with his much-loved third wife. But Mandela feels a sort of kinship with people living with AIDS. "There is no shame to disclose a terminal disease from which you are suffering and HIV is no different," he likes to say. "In prison, I suffered from tuberculosis and outside I suffered from cancer of the prostate. I went public in regard to both and nobody shunned me. We call upon everybody not to treat people who are HIV-positive with a stigma. We must embrace and love them."

Four-year-old AIDS orphan Andries in the orphanage ward at Kalfong Hospital in Pretoria. All of the orphans either have, or run the risk of developing, AIDS contracted from their deceased parents.

One of his moves was to use his old Robben Island prison number 46664, to raise money for the war on AIDS. 46664 is a worldwide music-led campaign to raise global awareness about HIV/AIDS and funds to fight the pandemic in Africa.

The first fundraising concert was held in Cape Town in 2003. It was not enough. In 2005, in a baseball cap, golf shirt and red AIDS ribbon, Mandela opened the second 46664 concert with his wife. "I am supposed to be retired," he told an audience of about 20,000 people. "I would love to enjoy the peace and quiet … but I can't rest easily while this beloved continent is being ravaged by a deadly epidemic." The crowd broke into the country's compromise national anthem – a trilingual hybrid of the beautiful traditional hymn "Nkosi Sikelele iAfrika" and the blustering Afrikaans of the apartheid-era anthem "Die Stem" – and stayed, despite the lashing rain. He raised ten million rands. The 46664 concert marking World AIDS Day on December 1 2007 also saw artists and ambassadors encouraging the stadium to take a stand against the pandemic.

The Nelson Mandela Children's Fund, which he started in 1995 to address the needs of young people facing homelessness, joblessness and poverty, now directs a large part of its resources where the country needs them most – AIDS orphans. The battle against HIV/AIDS has been central to Mandela's mission in recent years as he realizes that there is no way to tackle poverty without dealing with the virus. The Fund is his farewell gift to a nation, a continent and a world. It will carry on his work when he is no longer able to do so.

"AIDS today in Africa is claiming more lives than the sum total of all wars, famines and floods and the ravages of such deadly diseases as malaria," Mandela states. "We must act now for the sake of the world. AIDS is no longer a disease, it is a human rights issue."

The old man has much to look back on with pride. In his lifelong pursuit of integrity and dignity, he has almost never compromised and has tried never to humiliate his enemies. It has been a masterful, powerful, compelling performance as he moved from an aggressive, angry young man to a compassionate and forgiving elder statesman. South Africans have short memories and sometimes forget how close they came to civil war – not once, but several times. After many South Africans have

Celebrities join the cause at two 46664 concerts. Pictured are actor Will Smith with wife Jada Pinkett Smith, and singers Bono and Beyonce.

become accustomed to living in a relatively normal country, they forget how much effort it took to achieve that normality. Some even claim that they were better off under apartheid.

While most South Africans have moved on, the people who preferred apartheid still have the capacity to cause harm. In 2002, a series of midnight bomb blasts rocked Soweto, the sprawling township, now bigger than its mother city, Johannesburg. One woman was killed in her bed by falling debris when several of the bombs disrupted the railway links with Johannesburg. A mosque was wrecked. A day later, another bomb went off in the nearby capital city of Pretoria. The bombings were the most serious to hit the country since apartheid rule ended. They failed to change the force of history and create a coup, however.

By the end of the year, the police had detained more than two dozen right-wingers from a white, Christian paramilitary organization: the Boeremag. They also seized nearly 900 kilograms of explosives and several fire-arms caches. Half a century after Mandela's own Pretoria treason trial, South Africa had another. One of their targets, according to the state prosecutor, was Mandela himself.

A highly unimpressed newspaper editorial snorted at the cheek of it: "The whole nation has reason to be grateful that Mandela was its first post-apartheid president, and none more than the extreme right wing. Were it not for Mandela's extraordinary commitment to reconciliation and tolerance, they would hardly have been walking free these past nine years."

Twenty-two thousand victims of extraordinarily

Here, British model Naomi Campbell shares a seat with Mandela at a children's charity in Barcelona, 2001.

Mandela accepts the International Gandhi Peace Prize award for social, economic and political transformation, received from Indian president K.R. Narayanan in New Delhi. Mandela is the only person of non-Indian origin, besides Mother Teresa, to have won the award.

severe human rights abuses testified at the Truth and Reconciliation Commission hearings in the 1990s. Often, all they asked in return were small amounts of money: enough to erect a tombstone for a murdered loved one, or rebuild a small tin shack destroyed by vigilantes, or pay the school fees of the sons and daughters of the activists who went missing. They were disappointed when, years later in 2003, the government agreed on only a small 33 rands payout for the victims. The Truth and Reconciliation Commission head, Desmond Tutu, had recommended more, and complained about the

government dragging its feet. It seemed to some as though the government was in danger of forgetting about the incredible sacrifices made by many of its more obscure citizens. South Africa made the transition without outside government interference or international peace-keeping troops but this transition would not have been possible without the suffering of tens of thousands of families. Mandela, the architect of reconciliation, kept quiet. He was no longer President, and loyalty to his party runs deep.

Crime and corruption remain constant worries,

Leaders of the world attend a gala night at Westminster in London, in 2003. Mandela tries to encourage foreign policies based on human rights rather than short-term self-interests, and worries aloud that the global actions of nations such as the USA are tainted by a deep-seated, unexamined contempt for darker skins.

although, oddly, sometimes both appear worse because of another Mandela legacy: a free press is now able to pursue and reveal misbehaviour without being shut down by an outraged government.

Mandela has never enjoyed paperwork but loves to work with people. He coped easily with a number of issues which threatened to disrupt the nation, including the eventual break-up of the Government of National Unity after the man who released him from prison, F.W. de Klerk, walked out. Now the same party that put him in jail, the National Party, has been dissolved after losing badly at the last elections in 2004. Many of its current leaders remain in government in an agreement with the ruling party, happily serving the men they once allowed to rot in jail, working for an organization they once banned. Nobody bats an eyelid. South

Africans have become accustomed to paradoxes.

Internationally, Mandela has tried hard to encourage foreign policies based on human rights rather than short-term self-interests. He often criticizes "countries that play policemen of the world", and worries aloud that the global actions of nations such as the USA are tainted by deep-seated, unexamined contempt for darker skins. South Africa, the richest nation on the continent by far, has been instrumental in ending several wars and conflicts in Africa – although it has been difficult to use South Africa's own personal history as a one-size-fits-all model. While Mandela has been careful not to throw his weight around as leader of the biggest economic power in the region, mobile phones, fast-food franchises and air-conditioned shopping centres throughout Africa are often a sign of the end of apartheid, and the reunion of South Africa with its African brothers and sisters. But South African businessmen know what to expect now if they receive a call from Mandela: it will be a courteous but unmistakeable request for money for a good cause – a clinic, a school, an orphan who needs a school uniform. Business is expected to contribute to the building of a new nation.

Abroad, the former president of South Africa sometimes finds he is better known than his own beloved country: "If I get a blank look when I tell someone in a foreign country that I am from South Africa, I just add the magic word 'Mandela'. The person's face inevitably lights up with understanding – and pleasure." A South African businessman who went to Thailand discovered to his amazement that he was being introduced as a native of Mandela-land. Three South Africans teaching English in Japan utterly confused their high school students. "You can't be from the same country, you all look different," said the puzzled high school students. Their next lesson was about Mandela, and the Rainbow Nation.

Although international analysts eagerly predicted disaster when he refused to serve more than one term in power, Mandela insisted that the country needed a younger, more energetic leader and handed over control to his deputy, Thabo Mbeki, in a smooth changeover. "You don't lead by your position," he once said. "But by the strength of your ideas." It was a masterful stroke, and a powerful reminder on a continent where too many aging leaders cling to power at the expense of their people.

Mandela knows time passes swiftly. He had to drop earth on the coffin of his lifelong friend Oliver Tambo before their dream of democracy had come to flower. In 2003, he had to say farewell to one of his long-term prison companions, the man who had rescued him when he had first arrived as a friendless, penniless student in wartime Johannesburg. Walter Sisulu was buried the day before he would have turned 91. In one of the apartheid struggle's great love affairs, Sisulu's wife of 60 years wrote, "You were taken away by the evils of the past the first time, but I knew you would come back to me. Now the cold hand of death has taken

you and left a void in my heart." Mandela was fortunate to have strong friendships with these two remarkable men. But the time of the liberation giants is passing, he is the last of the three wise men and depends closely on his brilliant, compassionate wife Graça, whose commitment to Africa matches his own. He moves slowly, painfully, with the use of an ivory-coloured cane. But his mind is as sharp as the pangas used to cut sugarcane.

His first wife, Evelyn, died in 2004 at the age of 82. His former wife Winnie Madikizela Mandela

Electoral Commission officials stand among the 600 computers used to tally the votes in the 1999 election.

154

NELSON MANDELA

The first and second black presidents of South Africa. Here, in 1999, outgoing Mandela celebrates with new president Mbeki.

remains alive and active in the struggle. Flamboyant, extravagant, emotional, possessed of what one author called "superhuman courage", blessed (or cursed) as a constant source of fascination for journalists, Winnie continues to pick at her own party and her own ex-husband for not doing enough to alleviate the plight of South Africa's downtrodden. Her techniques for doing so are somewhat dubious: she was convicted of 42 counts of fraud in 2005 in connection with bank loans made to employees of the ANC Women's League, which she argued she only signed because she wanted to help the poor.

But the two seem to have come to some sort of understanding as they age. Winnie and her daughters attended a memorial service in Johannesburg after Makgatho, Mandela's only surviving son, died of

AIDS. And when Johannesburg offered Mandela, its most famous resident, the freedom of the city in 2005, Winnie was spotted with her arm around the shoulders of the woman now married to Mandela, Graça.

Ironically, in 2005, archivists uncovered a hidden trove of Mandela's love letters to Winnie that had been sent during his Robben Island years. An unknown prison official had sent them to the wrong branch of government for storage, where they languished until now. The 20-year-old boxes will be removed and audited by the Nelson Mandela Centre of Memory Project. Archivists say that there is still much to discover. A retired police detective whose job was to decode prisoners' messages hid dozens of letters from Mandela in notebooks on top

Mandela poses for the cameras among the 20,000 postcards and letters from people wishing him a good retirement.

of his wardrobe for 33 years. The letters had been confiscated during a raid on Mandela's cell in Robben Island in 1971 and sent to him by mistake after he retired. In one of those strange twists of fate, the man who kept the notebooks safe all those years met the former president for the first time in 1964. It was the world-famous Rivonia Trial, and Donald Card was giving evidence against Mandela!

But Mandela's legacy has been badly damaged by the news that Winnie's lawyer, who became his own confidant, has been secretly making millions out of the Mandela name.

Ismail Ayob, his trusted lawyer, shuffled papers in front of Mandela in 2001, and somehow managed to persuade him to sign away all rights to the Mandela name. Ayob then worked closely with a white businessman to conduct what is being called a

> "... people in the world's poorest countries ... remain trapped in the prison of poverty."

forgery: thousands of artworks bearing the Mandela handprint and using his signature, have been sold. The money was meant to go to the Mandela charities. Instead – although the lawyer insists that Mandela's surviving children have benefited – the money may never be recovered.

Once again, Mandela had been betrayed. "His habit was to put documents in front of me and give me a brief explanation. I relied on him, and I signed what he advised," says Mandela's statement. His spokeswoman Zelda la Grange confirmed that Mandela often signed documents brought to him by Ayob without studying them.

A court case is brewing. Already, the defensive

lawyer has claimed that Mandela has lost his mind, and is just a feeble old man who has been misinformed. The feeble old man is not impressed. Once more, he has returned to the legal arena to defend his rights, filing a lawsuit, and demanding a fully audited account of what has been done in his name.

There have been so many attempts by charlatans and frauds to cash in on the Mandela legacy that an intellectual property lawyer was hired last year to represent the Nelson Mandela Foundation. By early 2005, 65 cases were pending. The name Nelson Mandela will become a trademark by the end of the year in a last attempt to stop others jumping on the bandwagon.

The man himself, regardless of the court cases, will remain a legend. In February 2005, at the ripe old age of 86, he addressed a rally in Trafalgar Square in London, where the one-time prisoner was introduced to cheers as "president of the world". For years, as the home of the South African Embassy, the square had housed anti-apartheid protestors. Now the theme was different: "Make Poverty History".

Once again, Mandela had broken his promise to retire from public life. Here he was, a tall, slowly moving figure in black, topped with his favourite fur hat, leaning on a walking stick. His right arm was tied loosely with the anti-poverty campaign symbol, the white band.

"Massive poverty and obscene inequality are such terrible scourges of our time that they rank alongside slavery and apartheid as social evils," he said, slowly and clearly. The industrialized world is twice as rich as when he went into jail but now less than half as generous with its aid. AIDS has reduced the average age in many African countries to thirty-something years, but the global fund to fight the disease has only a quarter of the money it needs. Fourteen countries have been granted some debt relief, but ten of them still pay more on debt than they spend on healthcare.

"In this new century millions of people in the world's poorest countries remain in prison, enslaved and in chains. They are trapped in the prison of poverty," Mandela told the world. "It's time to set them free."

The first and second black presidents of South Africa. Here, in 1999, outgoing Mandela celebrates with new president Mbeki.

CHAPTER 11

"Nelson Mandela,
There Is No One Like You"

"Nelson Mandela, ga go yo o tshwanang le wena [there is no one like you]," sang the excited students in the Tswana language. They leapt from their seats at the University of Limpopo and began dancing, slamming the soles of their feet in rhythm against the tiled floor. Some shrieked with joy. It was a hot day in December 2009, and 91-year-old Mandela had arrived unexpectedly at the graduation of his grandson Zinhle Dlamini, his only grandchild to become a medical doctor. So the students spontaneously changed the words of the struggle-era song from "yena" (him) to "wena" (you).

It was a dynasty in action. As Mandela waved to the crowd, his famous ex-wife and former parliamentarian Winnie Madikizela Mandela began her keynote speech. One of their two daughters, Zenani, the mother of the newly qualified medical doctor, escorted Mandela slowly to his seat. Mandela's grandson Zinhle recited his Hippocratic Oath. Also present was Zenani's husband, businessman, aristocrat and former banker, Prince Thumbumuzi ("Muzi") Dlamini. He married Zenani in 1973 when she was still in high school, much to the frustration and fury of Mandela, who was then in prison and could do little to prevent his educational aspirations for his daughter from evaporating.

"My son comes from a family of scholars," boasted Dlamini, one of 210 children fathered by the late King Sobhuza the Second of the tiny kingdom of Swaziland, Africa's last absolute monarchy. "The discipline for school has been taken from Madiba in this family." But the singing, cheering students were focused not on the graduate, the speaker or the family members. Their attention was reserved for the thin, tall, stooped figure with the huge smile. Despite their reaction, Mandela said nothing to the students – except when he congratulated his grandson, now Dr Zinhle Dlamini.

In fact, Mandela has said almost nothing in public for years now. He made no public statement when reports surfaced in 2009 that another adult grandson, Eastern Cape traditional leader and politician Mandla Mandela, may have sold the international television rights to film part of his grandfather's funeral. As a Member of Parliament, this grandson has a constituency which includes the village of Qunu, Mandela's home village, where he is expected to be laid to rest after a week-long lying-in-state ceremony in the capital of Pretoria. Mandela also made no public statement when the same grandson was embroiled in a legal case over who had the right to stay in Mandela's old house in Soweto – a case that was as much about the tourist money to be made from the Mandela name as it was about rightful occupancy.

In some respects, this silence is nothing new. He has always preferred to deal with family matters out of the glare of the media. In retrospect, the fact that prison censors read every word he wrote to his family must have been deeply upsetting to such a reticent man. He certainly resisted having to speak publicly during his divorce case against Winnie Madikizela Mandela. Mandela's discretion sometimes irritates members of the media and lobbyists for various causes, who would prefer a more outspoken retired leader along the lines of former American President Bill Clinton or former United Nations Secretary General Kofi Annan.

Nelson Mandela meets children after they had performed during a lunch to benefit Mandela's Children's Foundation, April 2009, in Cape Town, South Africa.

Despite homes in Cape Town and Johannesburg, Mandela is most comfortable in rural villages like this one, Mqezweni, not far from where he grew up in the beautiful but poverty-stricken Eastern Cape region.

NELSON MANDELA

But there have been glimpses still of the public Mandela. In 2009, he voluntarily made two unexpected appearances at election campaign rallies hosted by the ruling African National Congress (ANC), even though the political party was in no danger of losing the national elections.

At one rally, held near his home in the poverty-stricken but beautiful Eastern Cape province, a stiff and fragile-looking Mandela was virtually hoisted on to the stage in an undignified movement that prompted considerable speculation about his health. At that rally, he downplayed his own appearance, preferring instead to favour the other main speaker, Jacob Zuma, who had just won a bruising and bitter

internal power battle with Thabo Mbeki, the man who succeeded Mandela as President, for the title of leader of the party. "Nxamalala [Jacob Zuma's Zulu clan name] has already spoken," Mandela told the crowd of thousands of rain-drenched supporters. "Mine is simply to greet you. Despite the rain, you have all come here in numbers to show your commitment to the ANC. May you live forever. Long live the ANC!"

He made no mention of the fact that the genial Zuma – who spent a decade with Mandela in prison on the notorious Robben Island under apartheid – had been acquitted in a rape case in which he admitted having unprotected sex with the HIV-

Nelson Mandela arrives at the final ANC election rally of the 2009 campaign.

positive daughter of a close friend. Nor did Mandela mention that Zuma had been under investigation for corruption in an episode which saw one of Zuma's close friends go to jail. Loyalty to the ANC was paramount. Naturally, he didn't mention that Zuma had been fired once as Deputy President as suspicions grew about his involvement in a multi-million-rand international arms sale scandal.

The problem with Mandela's silence is that it leaves him vulnerable to constant gossip. Allies of embattled ex-President Thabo Mbeki spread rumours that Mandela was appalled at infighting within the party and might not vote in elections. Others claimed that Mandela has a "soft spot" for Mbeki's rival, Jacob Zuma.

At another rally in Johannesburg, Mandela did not walk into the stadium but was driven around in a golf cart. Again, he was virtually carried up the steps to the podium, and carefully placed in an armchair near Jacob Zuma as a visual sign of support for the new and controversial leader. He did not give a live address, but a pre-recorded announcement was played instead, prompting some speculation that his speech was becoming erratic. "We must remember our primary task. It is to eradicate poverty and ensure a better life for all. The ANC has the historic responsibility to help build a united, non-racial society," the giant screens broadcast as chants of "Mandela, Mandela" rang out. It wasn't the kind of soul-stirring oratory that came from the man at the height of his powers. But in both cases, the brief speeches did demonstrate his loyalty to the ANC. Mandela has said that the first thing he will do after death, if and when he arrives in heaven, is look for the nearest ANC branch.

This attitude, some observers argue, is a problem. Is his loyalty to the ANC, to all South Africans or to human rights victims around the world? Despite benefiting from worldwide outrage over apartheid, the democratic South African government has been distinctly reluctant to get involved in equally messy human rights issues around the world.

The Nelson Mandela Anti-Apartheid Archive notes that international solidarity for "one person, one vote" in South Africa – solidarity which included embargoes on weapons sales, economic and financial sanctions, sports and cultural boycotts and

protests – was "arguably the biggest social movement the world has seen". However, even though the United Nations General Assembly announced in 2009 that Mandela's birthday (18 July), was to be known as "Mandela Day" to mark his contribution to world freedom, there are critics who say that Mandela has failed to use his international profile to champion the victims of human rights abuses whether they live nearby in Zimbabwe, or more distantly in Palestine or Burma.

Some analysts argue that Mandela had hoped to leverage his position and history in order to solve longstanding and complex problems elsewhere, such as Northern Ireland and Israel/Palestine. However, politicians and organizations embroiled in disputes outside of South Africa sometimes reacted with ill-disguised hostility to his interventions. It might be that Mandela was handicapped because he did not have any personal relationships with fellow leaders after so many years in jail. It is also true that there were many pressing needs keeping him at home: it was incredibly difficult to take over the reins of government from his reluctant predecessor, and South Africa had enormous problems of its own to tackle.

Mandela did have some successes internationally. Shortly after becoming president, Mandela attempted to help resolve the long-running dispute between the ANC's ally, Muammar Gaddafi of the North African state of Libya, and the United States and Britain, over the Lockerbie bombing. Mandela proposed South Africa as a venue for the trial of the two Libyans accused of sabotaging an aeroplane which then crashed at the Scottish town of Lockerbie in 1988, killing 270 people. (The Libyans were eventually tried and convicted in The Netherlands, not South Africa – but without Mandela's urging, it is not clear that the trial would have happened at all.)

However, Mandela's efforts to use his status to negotiate with the military general Sani Abacha, who then ruled Nigeria, failed. Mandela was criticised for his seeming loyalty to African leaders in the face of international pressure – and his ANC successors, Thabo Mbeki and Jacob Zuma, have been accused of continuing this trend. Mandela rejected calls for sanctions against Nigeria at a Commonwealth meeting in the hopes that this would offer him some bargaining power, but he was unable to save the life of environmental activist and author Ken Saro Wiwa and eight of his compatriots from Nigeria's Ogoni region, who were executed by the military. "Abacha is sitting on a volcano and I am going to explode it from under him," Mandela vowed. But nothing happened, and Mandela's international negotiations became fewer and fewer. Some analysts argue that he uses his position discreetly; others say that he does not use it at all.

In retirement, Mandela has been silent on a wide range of international issues, despite the efforts of organisations such as Open Shuhada Street, an international campaign with South African roots, which calls on the Israeli Government to open the street in Hebron in the West Bank to Palestinians rather than reserve it for Israelis and tourists. Many organisations have asked for Mandela's support, but his spokespersons normally refuse such requests, arguing that he is retired. However, Mandela speaks on behalf of the African National Congress during elections and he continues to appear in person to fundraise for his anti-HIV campaign, so it is not clear whether his silence is due to fatigue, illness or a desire to focus on problems close to home rather than international issues.

President Jacob Zuma speaks with Nelson Mandela, with former Zambian president Kenneth Kaunda in the background, February 2010.

Indeed, some South Africans resent any implication that Mandela must assist in international disputes. They believe that the international community must still do more to assist South Africa – and perhaps this is Mandela's view as well. Another struggle comrade from Robben Island prison, former Premier of Gauteng and businessman and lately Human Settlements Minister Tokyo Sexwale, addressed a parliamentary committee after the devastating 2010 earthquake which destroyed the capital city of Haiti – but not to rally support for the impoverished residents of the African diaspora or help the first black-run republic the world has seen. Rather, Sexwale complained that the international focus meant that there was less attention paid to South Africa. "We are dealing with a manmade disaster," he said, referring to evidence that the 300 squatter camps in South Africa at the time of the democratic changeover have mushroomed into over 2,500 informal settlements. "It is Haiti every day. The earth broke there. Here the earth didn't break, but the consequences are the same. It is a disaster," said Sexwale, who nonetheless denied that the democratically elected overnment bore responsibility for the housing shortage.

Meanwhile, as celebrities continue to queue for photographs with Mandela – including American movie actor Danny Glover and British comedian Eddie Izzard, who's raising funds for the Nelson Mandela Foundation – it is becoming more and more difficult for ordinary South Africans to have any physical contact with the great man. He only meets people who offer money, it seems. A lot of money. For example, for a one million rand donation to the Refurbishing Fund, which is repairing the Mandela house and acquiring Mandela's former offices and residence, you might expect a visit with the great man. However, the Nelson Mandela Foundation offers only a certificate signed by Nelson Mandela and a prominent "foundation donor" plaque displayed within the Centre.

Even if a donor offers two-and-a-half million rand towards the Foundation's dialogue series of lectures on AIDS, development, poverty, education, peace and reconciliation, the donation still only comes with a certificate signed by Nelson Mandela. In fact, according to the foundation's own website, only a

five million rand donation to the endowment fund will trigger a presentation of the signed certificate by Nelson Mandela himself. For a country in which anywhere from a third to half of all adults are unemployed, these figures can be difficult to understand.

Mandela's silence and isolation continues despite constant activity by old comrades such as South Africa's first black Anglican archbishop, Desmond Mpilo Tutu, another winner of the Nobel Peace Prize. Although nearly 80 years old, Tutu campaigns against AIDS and tuberculosis, poverty and racism. Although both Tutu and Mandela conduct much of their work through foundations, Tutu is much more active while Mandela allows his management to conduct their work on their own. Tutu also confronts South Africans on less popular issues, such as violent bigotry towards foreigners and a long-standing denial of African homosexuality, especially against African lesbians, in what is, after all, a deeply conservative country in many ways. Tutu, who

"It is Haiti every day. The earth broke there. Here the earth didn't break but the consequences are the same."

introduced the term Rainbow Nation to describe the country's diversity, clearly sees himself as a global activist. For example, Mandela spoke at the 2007 launch of The Elders, the influential group of retired leaders, and is credited with bringing them together. But Mandela has honorary status only, while Mandela's wife Graça Machel is an active member and Tutu chairs the organization.

Arguably, far too many of Mandela's public appearances in the last five years have been photo opportunities, taking advantage of his worldwide profile while strictly limiting any activities or input from "the old man", who now walks with the aid of a stick. It is Tutu who frequently initiates actions, sometimes with his fellow Nobel Peace Prize laureates, in support of long-term Burmese prisoner Aung San Suu Kyi and Tibetan Buddhist leader Dalai Lama. In contrast, the South African Government blocked the Dalai Lama's visit to the country to attend an anti-racism conference in 2010, in what was widely interpreted as sop to the powerful Chinese lobby which opposes Tibetan self-determination. At the time, Tutu spoke out; Mandela remained silent. Mandela remained silent when Tutu was viciously criticised by high-ranking Government figures when he noted flaws in the liberation movement in his speech at the annual Nelson Mandela Foundation lecture in 2004.

Other old colleagues have also been far more vocal than Mandela. These struggle veterans have also been able to admit their own flaws. For example, former exile and former Education Minister Kader Asmal, once lamented the fact that he had not spoken out more against Zimbabwean dictator Robert Mugabe, who has been protected in many ways by the South African Government. Mandela once said that he should have done more to speak out against HIV – but he has said nothing about his failure to prevent the economic and political destruction of Zimbabwe.

Then in March 2010, Asmal, now retired, spoke out against the increasingly militaristic approach of the new police commissioner, a former struggle activist, who demanded that he be addressed as general and sweeps through cities in a convoy of police vehicles, pushing other users off the roads. "We spent days and days in 1991 to get away from the idea of a militarized police force. It's extraordinary. This is a kind of craziness all of us have to take into account," Asmal said. Mandela, however, stayed silent.

There have been claims that Mandela's official silence is being used to conceal his deteriorating mental condition. The confusion over his health has given rise to a number of rumours, which have been exploited deliberately in some cases. In 2003,

Mandela's death was posted by mistake on the CNN website. In 2007, a fringe right-wing group distributed hoax email and mobile phone text messages claiming that the authorities had covered up Mandela's death and that white South Africans would be massacred after his funeral. Other reports suggest age-related dementia. February 2010 marked the 20th anniversary of his historic walk to freedom after being in jail for 27 years, but Mandela did little but pose in a chair for a photograph to mark the occasion. "Especially since his memory began to fail him, he has become more reclusive, protected by a staff that worries he might embarrass himself." So wrote former Johannesburg *New York Times* bureau

Mandela and his former wife Winnie Madikizela-Mandela toast the 20th anniversary of Mandela's release from prison, February 2010.

chief Bill Keller in 2009 in the USA.

Misunderstandings have occurred, such as one with British television presenter Jeremy Clarkson. Mandela appeared to be under the misapprehension that Clarkson's show was about astronauts rather than cars. Clarkson later said that the misunderstanding was explicable.

"Mr Mandela is as well as anyone can expect of someone who is 91 years old and who has lived an active and demanding life," said former academic, Jakes Gerwel, who chairs the Nelson Mandela Foundation, in 2009. At the same time, however, Gerwel said Mandela, who was treated with a seven-week course of radiation for prostate cancer

in 2001, "needs to rest more than he has in the past" and "therefore recently decided to cut back his engagements even further". This might explain why work on volume two of his autobiography has gone so slowly.

Two specific problems have arisen as a result of his silence – and perhaps also as a result of our desire for heroes. One is that people continue to use his name without permission. For example, there have been several cases of fraudsters linking the 2010 FIFA Football World Cup Award to Mandela. In one case, the scam announced a non-existent lottery win by email in order to try to gain access to people's bank accounts. Each fake email was printed over an image of Nelson Mandela holding the FIFA World Cup Trophy.

Other scams were linked to Mandela's 90th birthday or promise the opportunity for a handshake with the great man, warning in halting English: "Please be informed that you are not expected to disclose the award information to anybody until your winning fund is transferred to your nominated account, this is to avoid double claim that may hinder the process of your winning."

The other problem is that cutting back engagements while there is global hunger for the Mandela name has meant an increasing focus on his family. Mandela's family does not have his diplomatic skills. In 2010, during the countdown to the FIFA Soccer World Cup being held for the first time in Africa, a scandal erupted when the distinguished journalist, Lady Nadira Naipaul, published an interview with Mandela's ex-wife Winnie Madikizela Mandela in a British newspaper. In the interview, which allegedly took place months earlier in Soweto at Madikizela Mandela's home, his ex-wife said Mandela had been sidelined and was only trotted out as a "figurehead". "Look what they make him do. The great Mandela. He has no control or say any more," she said. "Mandela is now a corporate foundation. He is wheeled out globally to collect the money and he is content doing that." Madikizela Mandela also accused her former husband of going into jail as a revolutionary but coming out broken, saying "he let us down. He agreed to a bad deal for blacks." She even complained that their daughters had to "get through much red tape just to speak to their father."

NELSON
MANDELA
MUSEUM

The Nelson Mandela museum
in Umtata on the opening day.

NELSON MANDELA

Within days, Madikizela Mandela had denied the interview took place at all, although the *London Evening Standard* stood by the story and said they had a photograph of Winnie Madikizela Mandela with Nadira Naipaul.

Oddly enough, at the same time, Winnie Madikizela Mandela staked claim to the Mandela name, saying "Nobody owns Madiba (his clan name). Nobody, not even the ANC, which he and I love equally, can dispossess his family of the Mandela legacy." This statement left some observers wondering if there was a financial tussle going on for the Mandela name.

But what was interesting within South Africa was the groundswell of support for Winnie Madikizela Mandela's criticisms – whether she actually made them or not. On radio talk shows, through blogs and letters or mobile phone messages to newspaper editors, people said that they agreed with her complaints. One such writer, Ncedo Mahala, sent an email to a Johannesburg-based daily newspaper asking, "What is it that she said that is not already known? It's no secret that the gap between rich and poor in this country has grown so wide that it will take a miracle, not a government, to narrow it." In a text message printed in the national daily *The Times* on March 12, 2010, someone else observed: "It doesn't matter whether or not she was quoted correctly, what matters is that she fearlessly spoke the minds of millions of ordinary people."

In contrast, another anonymous text message accused Mandela's ex-wife of "wallowing in the gravy train", going on to say that "her kind have done nothing for hard-working South Africans since 1994

A protestor hurls a mattress as riots break out over inadequate housing and poor public services, July 2009, Mpumalanga, South Africa.

46664
's in our hands

[the first year of democracy] except take for themselves." But by far the overwhelming reaction was support for her criticism of Mandela. "Winnie said what most black people known and believe," said another text message.

So it would seem that Mandela's reputation as the great reconciler may be lost to growing dissatisfaction within South Africa from the poverty-stricken, predominantly black, working-class majority. Meanwhile, Mandela's international reputation may be tarnished by his refusal to intervene on human rights abuses, lest he embarrass his own government. His reputation remains strong, however, within South Africa's small but vocal middle class.

Is it not fair to allow someone so elderly, having had such a difficult life, to relax and enjoy his personal life? As long ago as 2004, his personal assistant Zelda la Grange said that Mandela was revelling in the freedom of being able to decide from day to day what he wanted to do with his time. He was taking great pleasure in revisiting places in Soweto he remembered from his younger days and spending time with his Mozambican-born wife, Graça.

So perhaps it is time for the next generation to take up his causes, rather than complain that he is no longer being a role model. After a lifetime devoted to the struggle for human rights, can we really begrudge the man some few moments of ordinary human happiness?

"We say tonight after nearly 90 years of life, it's time for new hands to lift the burdens," he said onstage at a 2008 fundraising concert in London's Hyde Park to celebrate his 90th birthday. "It's in your hands now."

NELSON MANDELA AT 90

THE CELEBRATION

Nelson Mandela smiles during the launch of postage stamps in Johannesburg, 2008, issued to celebrate his 90th birthday.

Index

Index

Acknowledgements

Mandela, Nelson. *Long Walk to Freedom* (Abacus, 1995)
Sampson, Anthony. *Mandela: The Authorised Biography* (Jonathan Ball, 1999)
Callinicos, Luli. *Oliver Tambo: Beyond The Engeli Mountains* (David Philip, 2004)
Sisulu, Elinor. *Walter and Albertina Sisulu – In Our Lifetime* (David Philip, 2003)

The publishers would like to thank the following sources for their kind permission to reproduce the pictures in the book.

3. Corbis/Reuters; 4. Getty Images/Gareth Davies; 6. Corbis/Peter Johnson; 8. Topfoto.co.uk/Louise Gubb/The Image Works; 10/11. Corbis/Gallo Images; 13. Rex Features/SIPA; 14. Rex Features/SIPA; 16 Getty Images/Per-Anders Pettersson; 17. Rex Features/SIPA; 18. Getty Images/ Hulton Archive; 20. Corbis/Bettmann; 21. Corbis/Hulton-Deutsch Collection; 22 Corbis/Bettmann; 24. Schadeberg Collection/Jurgen Schadeberg; 25. Schadeberg Collection/Jurgen Schadeberg; 26. Getty Images/Time Life Pictures; 27. Getty Images/Time Life Pictures; 28 Topfoto.co.uk; 29. Bailey's African History Archive; 30 Corbis/Reuters; 32. Schadeberg Collection/Jurgen Schadeberg; 34/35. Schadeberg Collection/Jurgen Schadeberg; 36. Corbis/Hulton-Deutsch Collection; 38. Topfoto; 39 Bailey's African History Archive (top & bottom);40. Mayibuye Centre; 41. Schadeberg Collection/Jurgen Schadeberg; 42/43 Schadeberg Collection/Jurgen Schadeberg; 44. Topfoto.co.uk ; 45. Corbis/Bettmann (top), Schadeberg Collection/Jurgen Schadeberg (bottom); 46: Schadeberg Collection/Bob Gosani; 48. Rex Features/SIPA; 49. Schadeberg Collection/Jurgen Schadeberg; 50. Topfoto.co.uk; 52/53. Getty Images/Hulton Archive; 55. Schadeberg Collection/Jurgen Schadeberg; 56. Topfoto.co.uk; 57. Corbis/KPA/ZUMA (top), Topfoto.co.uk (bottom); 59. Schadeberg Collection/Jurgen Schadeberg (top), Topfoto.co.uk (bottom); 60/61 Getty Images/Peter Magubane/Time Life Pictures; 62. Corbis/Louise Gubb/SABA; 63. Corbis/Louis Gubb/SABA; 64. Topfoto.co.uk; 66. Bailey's African History Archive; 67. Rex Features/XME; 68. Rex Features/Oksanen; 69. Corbis/Hulton-Deutsch Collection; 70. Empics/Alpha; 71. Topfoto.co.uk; 72. Corbis/Bettmann; 74/75. Getty Images/Huton Archive; 76. Topfoto.co.uk; 77. Topfoto.co.uk;

78. Getty Images/Hulton Archive; 80. Corbis/Gallo Images; 82. Rex Features/Julian Kuus/SIPA; 83. Topfoto.co.uk; 84/85. Topfoto.co.uk; 86. Topfoto.co.uk/Julia Cumes/The Image Works; 87. Topfoto.co.uk/Julia Cumes/The Image Works; 89. Topfoto.co.uk; 90. Corbis/Peter Turnely; 92/93. Getty Images/Hulton Archive; 94/95. Corbis/Louise Gubb/SABA; 96 Bailey's African History Archives; 97. Corbis/Selwyn Tait/SYGMA; 98/99. Corbis/Bettmann; 100. Empics/PA; 102/103. Corbis/Patrick Durand/SYGMA; 105. Corbis/Gideon Mendel; 106/107. Corbis/Gideon Mendel; 108. Empics ; 109. Corbis/Peter Turnely; 110/111. Topfoto.co.uk/The Image Works 112. Corbis/Gideon Mendel; 113 Corbis/Louise Gubb; 114. Corbis/David Turnley; 115. Corbis/David Turnley; 117. Corbis/Greg Marinovich/SYGMA (top), Getty Images/Peter Magubane/Time Life Pictures (bottom); 118/119. Corbis/Reuters; 120/121 Corbis/Reuters; 122. Getty Images/Greg Marinovich; 123. Corbis/Joao Silva/SYGMA; 124. Topfoto.co.uk/Louise Gubb/The Image Works; 126/127.Topfoto.co.uk; 128/129. Corbis/SYGMA; 130/131. Corbis/Peter Turnley; 132. Topfoto.co.uk; 133. Empics/EPA; 134/135. Corbis/Louise Gubb/SABA; 136. Corbis/Reuters; 137. Rex Features/SIPA; 138. Corbis/Gideon Mendel (top), Empics/Matthew Fearne/PA (bottom); 139. Getty Images/AFP; 140. Corbis/Peter Magubane/SYGMA; 141. Corbis/Patrick Durand/SYGMA; 142/143. Topfoto.co.uk; 144. Corbis/Gideon Mendel; 146. Empics/ShayneRobinson/EPA; 147. Empics/Canada Press; 148. Corbis/Mike Hutchings/Reuters (left), Getty Images (right); 149. Corbis/Reuters; 150/151. Empics/EPA; 152. Corbis/Reuters; 153. Empics/EPA; 154. Rex Features/ Mykel Nicolaou; 155. Empics/EPA; 156/157. Corbis/Mike Hutchings/Reuters; 158. Getty Images/Chris Jackson; 160/161. Rex Features/Markus Zeffler; Press Association Images/Themba Hadebe/AP; 163. Getty Images/Gallo Images; 164/5. Press Association Images/Debbie Yazbek/AP; 166. Getty Images/Gallo Images; 167. Getty Images/Gareth Davies; 168/169. Reuters/Juda Ngwenya; 172/173. Reuters/Siphiwe Sibeko.

Every effort has been made to acknowledge correctly and contact the source and /or copyright holder of each picture, and Carlton Books apologises for any unintentional errors or omissions, which will be corrected in future editions of this book.